Expanded Blues Guitar

Traditional and Contemporary styles

Featuring 11 song transcriptions from the authors' album "Black Market Hearts"

Copyright © 2014 by Mark Wein

All rights reserved. This book or any portion thereof may not be reproduced or used in any manner whatsoever without the express written permission of the publisher except for the use of brief quotations in a book review or scholarly journal.

First Printing: 2014
ISBN: 978-0-578-13616-5

Mark Wein Music
211 W Katella Ave Suite B
Orange, CA 92867

www.MarkWeinGuitarLessons.com

For Mrs. Wein, who has supported me and put up with my crazy ideas all of these years.

Acknowledgements

A special thanks to everyone who participated or supported the making of both this book and the album that inspired it.

Scott Francisco
Martin Torres
Tyler Walton
Gary Pritchard
Tommy Harkenrider
Mark McFeely
Scheila Gonzalez
Sean Billlings
Cover Design by Kimball Illustration and Design
Sundel Perry Photography for the cover photographs on both this book and the album.

Each of the guys who contributed $100 each towards the production of the album to become part of the crew of the Thunderdome.

Everyone else who threw money or other means of support at this project to help it become a reality.

The online community at MarkWeinGuitarLessons.com/forums

The staff and customers of Premier Music

Contents

Section 1 - Blues Basics 8

Understanding Chord Progressions..9
Rhythmic Feels for Blues...10
12 Bar Blues..12
Using Capos to Play the Blues..14
Turnarounds and Quick Changes..15
Slow Blues Turnarounds...16
Turnarounds Used as Endings..17
QuickChanges..18
The "Three Phrase" concept for 12 bar blues...............................19
Common Movable Chord Voicings..22
Top and Bottom Parts for a 12 Bar Blues......................................23
A slighty more complicated top part over the same bottom..........25
Sliding 9ths!..26
Box Shuffles..28
The Boogaloo...29
Latin Blues or the "Blues Mambo"...30
Eight Bar Blues..31
Minor Blues..33

Section 2 - Scales and a little bit of Theory 36

How I am presenting the lead guitar material in this book............37
The CAGED System..38
Root Patterns from the CAGED System..39
Minor Pentatonic..40
Blues Scale..41
Major Triads...42
Major Scale..43
Major Pentatonic..44
Mixolydian Scale..45
Dominant 7th Chord Tones..45
The "3 phrase" approach to soloing..47
Chromatics and Chords Tones for Dominant Chords...................48

Section 3 - Song Transcriptions...51

Extended Scale Patterns..52
I'm Gonna Leave...53
Primer page for Someone Elses' Fool..60
Oblique Bends and Hybrid Picking..62
Someone Else's Fool...63
Roar..74
Can I Take You Home?..86
Scott's Guitar Part on "Can I Take You Home?"...89
Life is Good..92
Black Market Hearts..96
Steamrolled..101
Pop!...105
Everything's Cool...112
Toms' Guitar Part for "Everythings' Cool"..120
Rhythm Guitar for "The Last Time"...122
The Last Time - Solo Examples..124
The Last Time - Acoustic Guitar...125
The Last Time...126
Subterrania (The Prize)...136

How to use this book.

The first section is my attempt at teaching many of the basic concepts for Blues music that I think a guitarist should know....we have examples of styles and grooves, different ways that you can find structure in a blues, turnaround licks and all kinds of stuff like that. There is not much "lead guitar" in this section, but I want to teach what it is we guitar players are supposed to do the other 99% of the time we are on stage. This section covers more of the "traditional" electric blues that I might play on a gig and is perfect for Guitarists who are just getting their feet wet playing blues music or who would like to expand their knowledge.

The second section has scales, chords and tips on soloing. This is not really a soloing book for total beginners but I'm assuming that most of you already play a bit already and these are some of the things that I like to use that you might not find elsewhere - it is more of a reference for you to be able to find these sounds across the fretboard.

The third section has all of the song transcriptions from the album and lessons based on what I am doing as far as soloing or if there is a specific rhythm guitar idea that is not covered in the first section. I'll also talk about any kind of genre-twisting we might have done in any of the songs.

Go to http://markweinguitarlessons.com/forums/ for access to the additional PDF, mp3 and video files. There is a private forum for you to ask questions or discuss the book material. Once you have registered for the forum email me at markwein@markweinguitarlessons.com and include the word "**blackmarkethearts2014**" in your email along with your username for the forum and I'll get you access to all of the extras. I have streaming audio from the album and downloadable backing tracks as well as expanded lessons that would not fit in the final version of the book so it's well worth the time to check it out!

Introduction - Welcome to whatever this has become. (Skip ahead if you're not a fan of backstories)

I'm actually not kidding at this point. Almost two years ago I decided that I wanted to record an album of music that I enjoy playing (as opposed to playing other musicians music for other people to enjoy) so I gathered all of my favorite musician buddies together and asked if they would play on or produce an independently produced album of my music. And lucky for me they all said "yes".

I sat down to write some music for us to play and it turns out that I like playing Blues music in all of its various colors more than anything else at this point in my life so a contemporary blues album was born. The basic concept behind the album was that I wanted every song to be some kind of blues but that it shouldn't be the same as every other record out there and every song should have a fairly interesting and different groove. There are no Chicago-style 12 bar shuffles on this album as much as I enjoy doing that sort of thing on gigs. There is no slow 12/8 blues like "Stormy Monday" or "Texas Flood" on this album. I really tried to avoid the cliches that albums made by guitar players who grew up playing rock music first always seem to have.

On the other hand, there are traces of Rock, Funk, New Orleans Second Line, Latin and even Country music on this album. We recorded 17 songs ("Roar" was recorded twice, starting life as more of a Jerry Lee Lewis rocker before I came up with what you'll hear on the album) and I picked the 11 songs that I thought made the best collection of songs for an album. Most of what was left off were tunes that were too rock and roll, a Jump Blues song named after my dog or songs just plain not good enough to stand with the rest of the music.

Now we come to the part where this book starts to become a "thing". Every time I've recorded an album I've made a 3 ring binder where I keep music, lyrics, schedules, notes or whatever. This time around it was going to be a practice diary where I just logged what I worked on so that I could sharpen my chops before recording time. After a few rehearsals were recorded I found a few solos I liked that I transcribed so that I would remember the good bits. Then I charted a few tunes to make rehearsals more efficient. Before long there was a ton of stuff in the book and it was nice to go through it every once in a while and review ideas or get back on track with my practicing.

Right before we started actually recording I decided that I would try a crowd-funding website called Kickstarter. Essentially you post a campaign for a project and try to get people to pledge money to help you get the project funded. If you get enough pledges (you set an amount for the campaign) then you get funded. You offer enticements for people to contribute like free CD's, t-shirts or other swag or even live performances. One of the prizes I offered was the practice diary for $100. I figured someone might be interested in a book full of guitar licks.

It turned out that six people ended up ponying up $100 a piece for the book.

I worked it out where the first person who pledged gets the physical book but everyone else gets a much nicer version of it that has been done in notation software (so its legible) and I threw out the idea that I'll transcribe the whole album for it as well. Maybe I could turn some of the tunes into lessons for video later but there were no plans to actually write a real book until I realized that I was going to essentially write an entire book anyway.

For various reasons the recording process went from an estimated 4 months to over a year so I decided to put up a private forum for the folks who contributed and I just started posting PDF's and mp3s of the music as I got it since I was feeling bad about taking money and not giving anything in a reasonable amount of time. It was also a nice place to get feedback on what I was doing and one of the questions was about the book itself...

"As I've worked on this I've kinda started thinking that instead of just a book of transcriptions maybe I could do a book that has all of the songs in it but then have a section of basic blues theory and stylistic information and then some bits about how I've mangled that stuff in my own music. Rhythm and lead guitar lessons. Or maybe just a transcription book and a separate lesson book with only a few of the songs for examples in it.

What do you guys think?

The answer from pretty much everyone was that they thought the lesson book was the best idea and I realized that I could have a text to teach from for my students who wanted to play blues and possibly even cross-promote the album. Win-win!!!

In the process I've had a great time writing this (almost as much fun as making the album itself) and I hope you enjoy the book an the music that it is based on.

-Mark

Section 1

• • •

Basic Concepts, Styles and Guitar Parts for Blues

Understanding Chord Progressions

We have two or three basic chord progressions that form the core of most blues music, but before we learn them we need to understand a little bit about how chord progressions work.

We refer to a 12 Bar Blues as a "One, Four, Five" chord progression. The numbers are referring to the distances that the chords are from each other in a Major key. When we talk about playing chords in a Major key we are referring to chords that are only made up of notes in one Major scale.

Here is a C Major Scale spelled out:

Notes	C	D	E	F	G	A	B
Scale Degree	1	2	3	4	5	6	7
Roman Numeral	I	ii	iii	IV	V	vi	vii°
Chord in C Major	C	Dm	Em	F	G	Am	B diminished

"C" is the first note in the C scale, "D" is the second note in the C scale, "E" is the third note in the C scale and so on...what we call the "One" chord is a chord built off of the 1st note in the scale, or "C". The "Four" chord is built off of the 4th note in the scale ("F") and the "Five" chord is built on "G".

I won't do a full lesson on diatonic harmony here (which is how we find out what chords belong in what keys) but I think that this will get the idea across for our purposes. What IS important to know is this:

In a Major key the chords built off of the first, fourth and fifth notes will always be Major chords.

The chords built from the second, third and sixth notes will always be Minor chords.

A chord built from the seventh note will be Diminished.

You will also see the word "diminished" replaced with the " ° " symbol. For example we will use "A°" for the "A diminished" chord.

When we write chord progressions we use Roman Numerals to designate the chord relative to the 1st note or "Tonic". "I" is one, "IV" is four and "V" is five. We use upper case Roman Numerals for Major chords and lower case Roman Numerals for the minor chords. One thing any aspiring blues musician should do is start memorizing the I, IV and V chords for as many keys as possible although the first five or six of these will end up being the majority of the keys you will play as a guitarist. I've highlighted the "important" chords for you in this chart:

I	ii	iii	IV	V	vi	vii°
C	Dm	Em	F	G	Am	B°
G	Am	Bm	C	D	Em	F#°
D	Em	F#m	G	A	Bm	C#°
A	Bm	C#m	D	E	F#m	G#°
E	F#m	G#m	A	B	C#m	D#°
B	C#m	D#m	E	F#	G#m	A#°
F	Gm	Am	B♭	C	Dm	E°
B♭	Cm	Dm	E♭	F	Gm	A°
E♭	Fm	Gm	A♭	B♭	Cm	D°
A♭	B♭m	Cm	D♭	E♭	Fm	G°
D♭	E♭m	Fm	G♭	A♭	B♭m	C°

Rhythmic Feels for Blues

One of the most overlooked elements of music by many guitarists that I run into either as students or at jams is the concept of rhythm. I am assuming that if you are working out of this book that you can already play some guitar and know something of time and rhythm but I want to make sure that we understand the different between straight and shuffled eighth notes.

Straight Eighth Notes are evenly spaced subdivisions of the beat. In this case we are dividing each beat into two halves - the "down beat" which is the first half that we count the number of the beat on and the "up beat" which is the second half of the beat and is counted as the word "and". Try clapping the rhythm below with a metronome set to 60 beats per minute. Tap your foot on the metronome click, count "one and two and three and four and" out loud and then clap on every eighth note. The "ands" should happen directly between clicks and if you are tapping your foot on the downbeat the foot will be heading up (or at least not tapping again) on the upbeat. The foot tapping is to help you internalize the feeling of consistent time, which is really important for both your lead and rhythm playing.

Shuffled Eighth Notes are not as even feeling. The downbeat in a shuffle is actually felt longer than the upbeat. One way to show you how that feels is to demonstrate the triplet feel that the shuffle is based on.

A triplet is a group of three eighth notes crammed into a single beat where only two would normally go. We count them "**One**-trip-let **Two**-trip-let **Three**-trip-let **Four**-trip-let". Try just counting that out loud with the metronome before doing the exercise below. Then try clapping the top line of the music while counting out loud and tapping your foot on the beat like we did above.

The trick with this is that once you have the triplets mastered we are going to still count them but just clap on the down beat and the "let". That is what the bottom line of the example below is showing you. That will give you an actually shuffled (or "swing") eighth note rhythm.

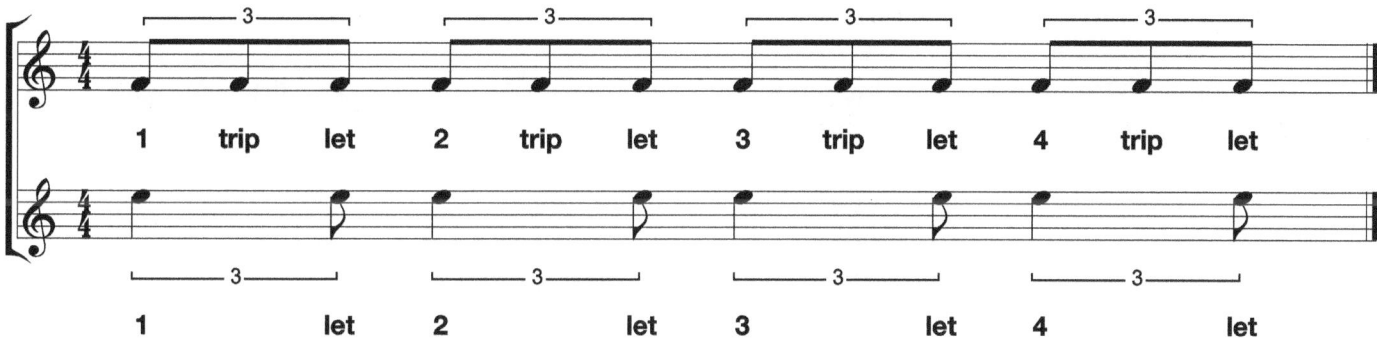

When we write a shuffled rhythm in this book the music will look like straight eighth notes but will have this symbol at the beginning which will tell you to play the eighth notes shuffled and not straight:

Dominant Chords in Blues

In most blues music the I, IV and V chords will be played as *Dominant Seventh* chords. In C that would give you C7, F7 and G7. In the Roman Numerals it would be written as I^7, IV^7 and V^7. We can also substitute 9th, 6th and 13th chords depending on the context but we'll explore that idea later.

12 Bar Blues

This is a chord progression that is 12 measures long. Certain chords need to happen in specific measures of that progression for it to be considered a blues progression.

One really good way of memorizing or "internalizing" this idea (or any of these progressions) is to learn it on paper or verbally first. Try this:

I chord for 4 measures

IV chord for 2 measures

I chord for 2 measures

V chord for one measure

IV chord for one measure

I chord for two measures

I try to get my students to be able to tell me from memory what the chord changes in a progression are before they play it. If you are reading it from a paper, trying to change chords when you hear certain lyrics or just guessing at it you will never really know where you are in the song. KNOW IT BEFORE YOU PLAY IT. Recite the the progression in bold above until you have it memorized.

A "chorus" or verse of blues is one time through the 12 bar progression. A song might have two verses (or choruses) of singing, a couple of choruses of solos and then another chorus or two of singing to wrap it up. In a sense the 12 bar form is a basic building block for a blues tune and we can put together a song pretty quickly if you know the feel, key and some basic alterations to the progression that we might want to include. These are not mandatory but are pretty common ideas.

Understanding Chord Progressions

We have two or three basic chord progressions that form the core of most blues music, but before we learn them we need to understand a little bit about how chord progressions work.

We refer to a 12 Bar Blues as a "One, Four, Five" chord progression. The numbers are referring to the distances that the chords are from each other in a Major key. When we talk about playing chords in a Major key we are referring to chords that are only made up of notes in one Major scale.

Here is a C Major Scale spelled out:

Notes	C	D	E	F	G	A	B
Scale Degree	1	2	3	4	5	6	7
Roman Numeral	I	ii	iii	IV	V	vi	vii°
Chord in C Major	C	Dm	Em	F	G	Am	B diminished

"C" is the first note in the C scale, "D" is the second note in the C scale, "E" is the third note in the C scale and so on...what we call the "One" chord is a chord built off of the 1st note in the scale, or "C". The "Four" chord is built off of the 4th note in the scale ("F") and the "Five" chord is built on "G".

I won't do a full lesson on diatonic harmony here (which is how we find out what chords belong in what keys) but I think that this will get the idea across for our purposes. What IS important to know is this:

In a Major key the chords built off of the first, fourth and fifth notes will always be Major chords.

The chords built from the second, third and sixth notes will always be Minor chords.

A chord built from the seventh note will be Diminished.

You will also see the word "diminished" replaced with the " ° " symbol. For example we will use "A°" for the "A diminished" chord.

When we write chord progressions we use Roman Numerals to designate the chord relative to the 1st note or "Tonic". "I" is one, "IV" is four and "V" is five. We use upper case Roman Numerals for Major chords and lower case Roman Numerals for the minor chords. One thing any aspiring blues musician should do is start memorizing the I, IV and V chords for as many keys as possible although the first five or six of these will end up being the majority of the keys you will play as a guitarist. I've highlighted the "important" chords for you in this chart:

I	ii	iii	IV	V	vi	vii°
C	Dm	Em	F	G	Am	B°
G	Am	Bm	C	D	Em	F#°
D	Em	F#m	G	A	Bm	C#°
A	Bm	C#m	D	E	F#m	G#°
E	F#m	G#m	A	B	C#m	D#°
B	C#m	D#m	E	F#	G#m	A#°
F	Gm	Am	B♭	C	Dm	E°
B♭	Cm	Dm	E♭	F	Gm	A°
E♭	Fm	Gm	A♭	B♭	Cm	D°
A♭	B♭m	Cm	D♭	E♭	Fm	G°
D♭	E♭m	Fm	G♭	A♭	B♭m	C°

Rhythmic Feels for Blues

One of the most overlooked elements of music by many guitarists that I run into either as students or at jams is the concept of rhythm. I am assuming that if you are working out of this book that you can already play some guitar and know something of time and rhythm but I want to make sure that we understand the different between straight and shuffled eighth notes.

Straight Eighth Notes are evenly spaced subdivisions of the beat. In this case we are dividing each beat into two halves - the "down beat" which is the first half that we count the number of the beat on and the "up beat" which is the second half of the beat and is counted as the word "and". Try clapping the rhythm below with a metronome set to 60 beats per minute. Tap your foot on the metronome click, count "one and two and three and four and" out loud and then clap on every eighth note. The "ands" should happen directly between clicks and if you are tapping your foot on the downbeat the foot will be heading up (or at least not tapping again) on the upbeat. The foot tapping is to help you internalize the feeling of consistent time, which is really important for both your lead and rhythm playing.

Our first playing example is a 12 bar blues in the key of A. We are playing the 8th notes with a shuffle feel and the actual part is what we call (depending on the part of the U.S. that you are from) a "Jimmy Reed", a "Lump", a "Grinder", a "Spread" or any of a bunch of names that people have come up with over the last 60-70 years.

I have written this in the open position because that is the easiest way to play a 12 bar blues for the first time. It is also the most traditional way to play a 12 bar blues in A. Later on we will discuss closed positions and using a capo to play in other keys.

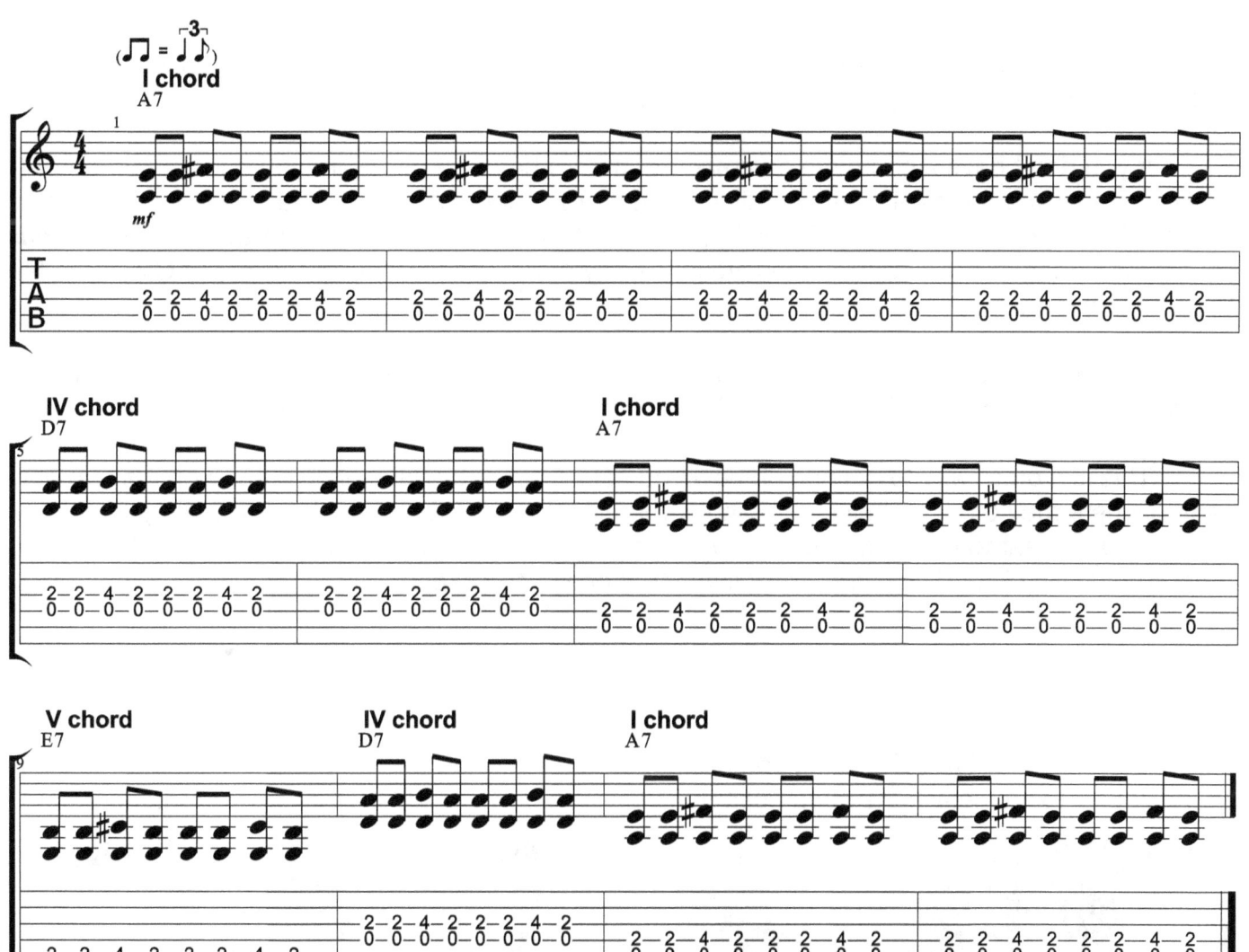

13

Using Capos to Play the Blues

Originally when I first started playing guitar the teacher that I was studying with had resented the capo as something of a crutch and impressed on me the need to learn my fretboard and moveable chord shapes like barre chores, power chords and movable jazz chord voicings. As I played more original rock music I discovered that the capo was a great way to arrange guitar parts by doings things such as allowing one guitarist to play a G barre chord at the 3rd fret and the other to play somthing like a D major open chord shape with the capo at the 5th fret. The difference in timbre really made the difference in a recording or even live in two guitar bands. Sometimes it just plain sounds really cool.

As far as playing blues goes I wasn't hip to the idea that many of the Chicago electric blues players had come from acoustic blues backgrounds where using a capo was an important tool. Then it became easier to play many of the great ideas I had heard from open position keys like E and especially A in other keys by moving the capo up the fretboard.

If you don't have a complete command of the fretboard at this point you can at least determine what key you are playing in by finding the note the capo plays on the 5th string if you are playing your ideas from the examples in the key of A. Put the capo at the second fret and now the music you've learned from the last few pages are in the key of B. The third fret is the key of C and the 5th fret is the key of D.

For ideas that use the key of E in the open position (of which we haven't done yet in this book) the first fret is the key of F, the 3rd fret is the key of G and the 5th fret is the key of A.

This is a great way to change up how you sound either by yourself in a band or in a two guitar setting where they other guitarist is playing something more "normal" in standard tuning. Open tunings would be neat to hear but this is an area that I am not enough of an expert to cover in this book other than a few cliched slide riffs so I'll leave that one to the experts.

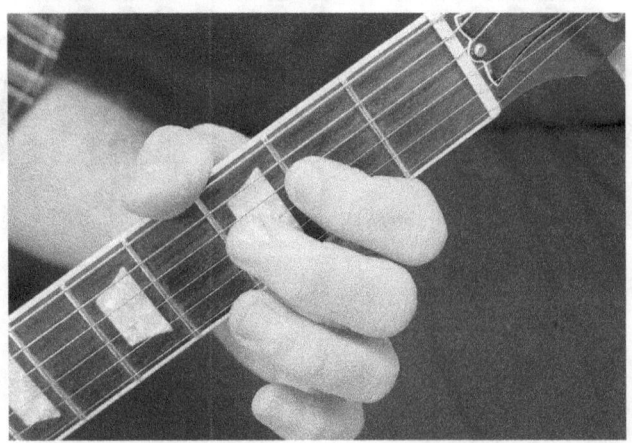

Playing the A5 chord (the first thing you play in the shuffle examples) in the open position.

Playing the A5 chord with the capo on the 2nd fret, making it a B5 chord.

Our first playing example is a 12 bar blues in the key of A. We are playing the 8th notes with a shuffle feel and the actual part is what we call (depending on the part of the U.S. that you are from) a "Jimmy Reed", a "Lump", a "Grinder", a "Spread" or any of a bunch of names that people have come up with over the last 60-70 years.

I have written this in the open position because that is the easiest way to play a 12 bar blues for the first time. It is also the most traditional way to play a 12 bar blues in A. Later on we will discuss closed positions and using a capo to play in other keys.

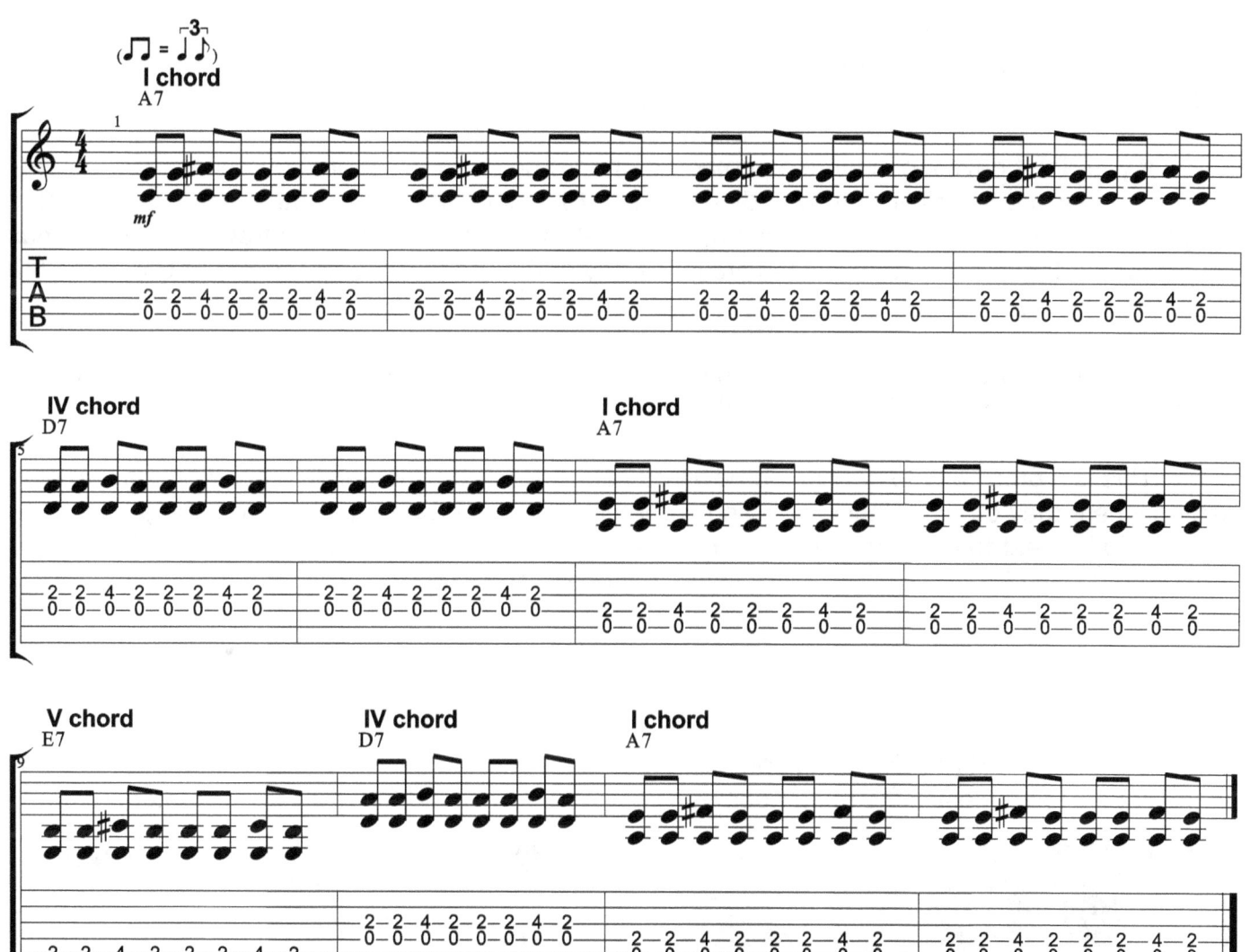

Using Capos to Play the Blues

Originally when I first started playing guitar the teacher that I was studying with had resented the capo as something of a crutch and impressed on me the need to learn my fretboard and moveable chord shapes like barre chores, power chords and movable jazz chord voicings. As I played more original rock music I discovered that the capo was a great way to arrange guitar parts by doings things such as allowing one guitarist to play a G barre chord at the 3rd fret and the other to play somthing like a D major open chord shape with the capo at the 5th fret. The difference in timbre really made the difference in a recording or even live in two guitar bands. Sometimes it just plain sounds really cool.

As far as playing blues goes I wasn't hip to the idea that many of the Chicago electric blues players had come from acoustic blues backgrounds where using a capo was an important tool. Then it became easier to play many of the great ideas I had heard from open position keys like E and especially A in other keys by moving the capo up the fretboard.

If you don't have a complete command of the fretboard at this point you can at least determine what key you are playing in by finding the note the capo plays on the 5th string if you are playing your ideas from the examples in the key of A. Put the capo at the second fret and now the music you've learned from the last few pages are in the key of B. The third fret is the key of C and the 5th fret is the key of D.

For ideas that use the key of E in the open position (of which we haven't done yet in this book) the first fret is the key of F, the 3rd fret is the key of G and the 5th fret is the key of A.

This is a great way to change up how you sound either by yourself in a band or in a two guitar setting where they other guitarist is playing something more "normal" in standard tuning. Open tunings would be neat to hear but this is an area that I am not enough of an expert to cover in this book other than a few cliched slide riffs so I'll leave that one to the experts.

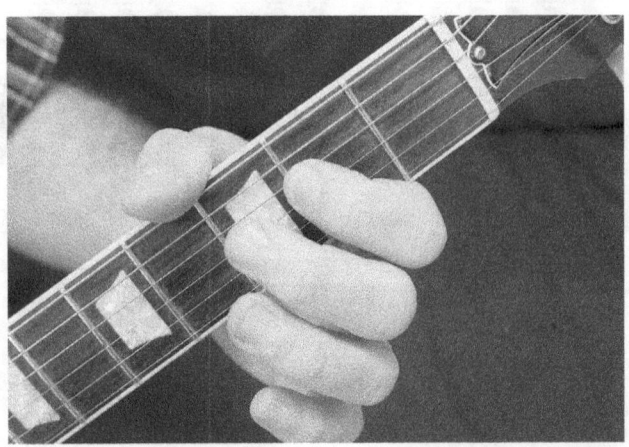

Playing the A5 chord (the first thing you play in the shuffle examples) in the open position.

Playing the A5 chord with the capo on the 2nd fret, making it a B5 chord.

Turnarounds

Turnarounds are usually played in the last two bars of a 12 or 8 bar chord progression. Turnaround licks will typically consist of a lick in the 11th bar and the V chord played in the 12th bar. That V chord at the end of a 12 bar progression makes us feel like we need to start back at the top of the progression. Here are several turnaround ideas to play with in the key of A - I will have more examples in the online shuffle examples:

1.

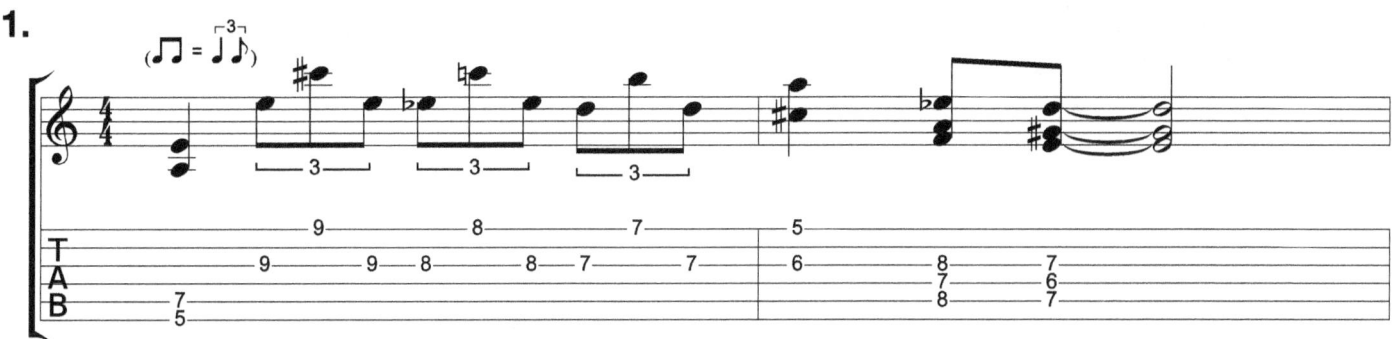

2.

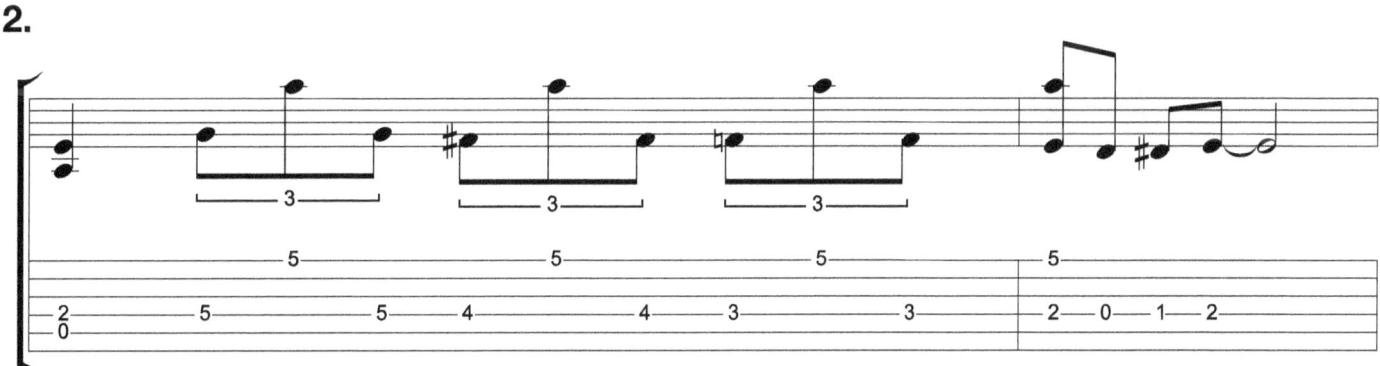

3.

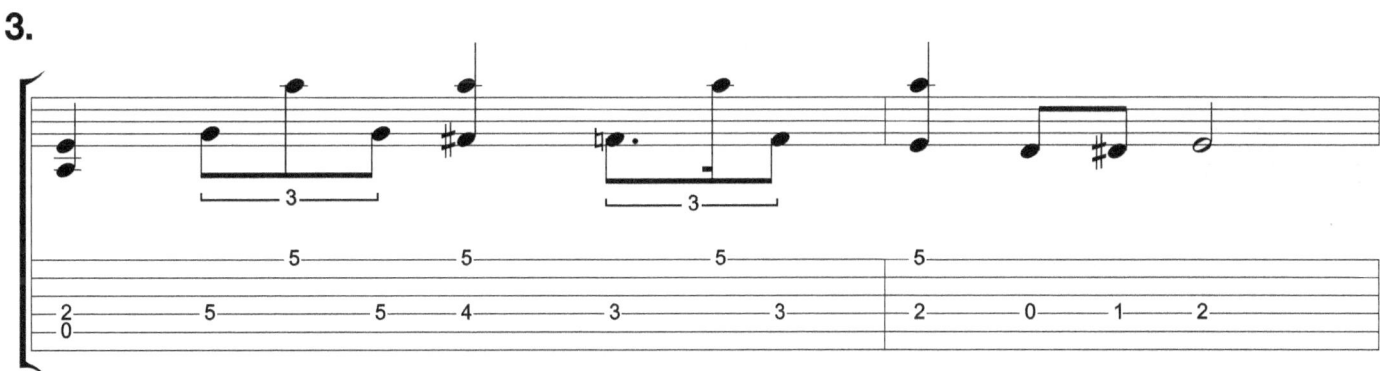

4.

Turnarounds used as Endings

One common way to end a 12 or 8 bar blues is to replace the last chord of a turnaround lick with the I chord (or a bII (flat two) chord into the I chord). While the V chord in a turnaround makes you feel like you need to start the form all over again the I chord will actually end or resolve the progression. I have two standard turnaround licks on this page with the endings altered this way that are shuffled and the third example is from my song "I'm Gonna Leave", which has a straight eighth note feel. Try altering any other turnarounds that you might know to make them endings. Each of the following ending ideas are in the key of A - try them with the 12 bar blues examples!

1.

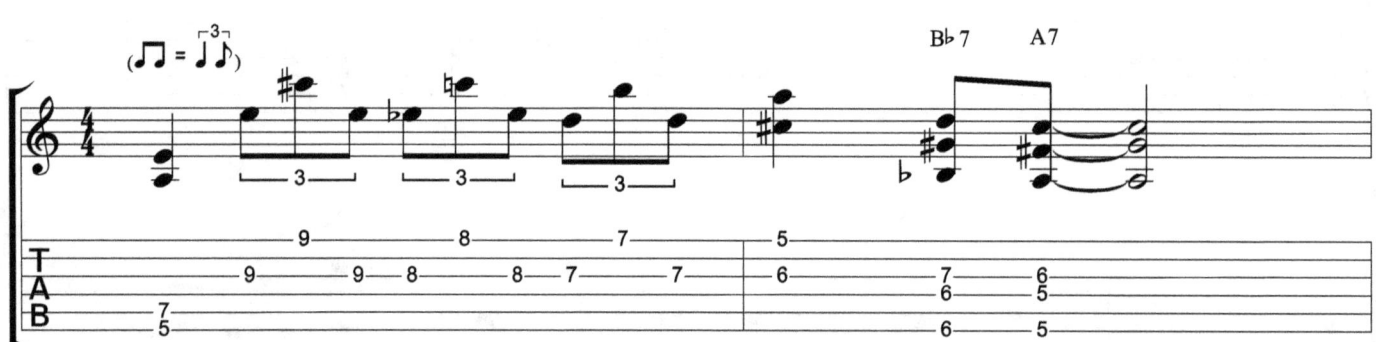

2.

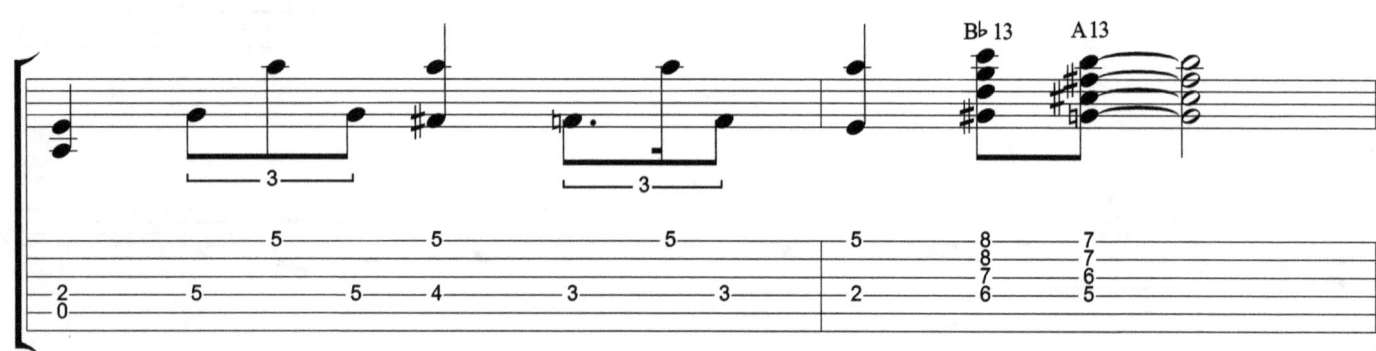

3.

Slow Blues Turnarounds

Sometimes in a slower blues you might see the last two measures look more like this:

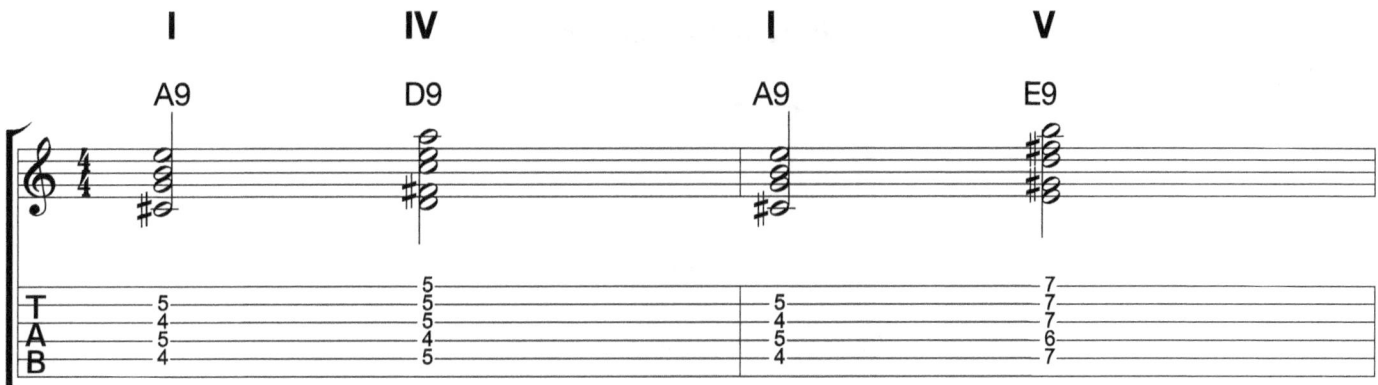

Over that chord progression I might play something like one of these turnaround ideas:

This one I stole from a live recording of Kid Ramos playing a slow blues at a jam session. It is in the key of B:

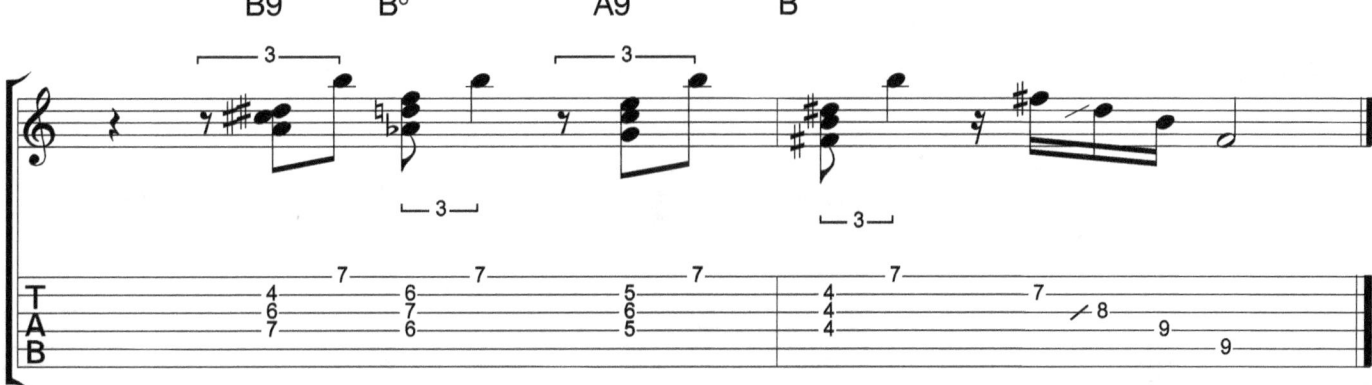

Quick Changes

In some songs (usually slower ones) we can play a "quick change", where we will put a IV chord in the second measure and then continue on with the chord progression as before:

I chord for 1 measures

IV chord for 1 measures

I chord for 2 measures

V chord for one measure

IV chord for one measure

I chord for two measures

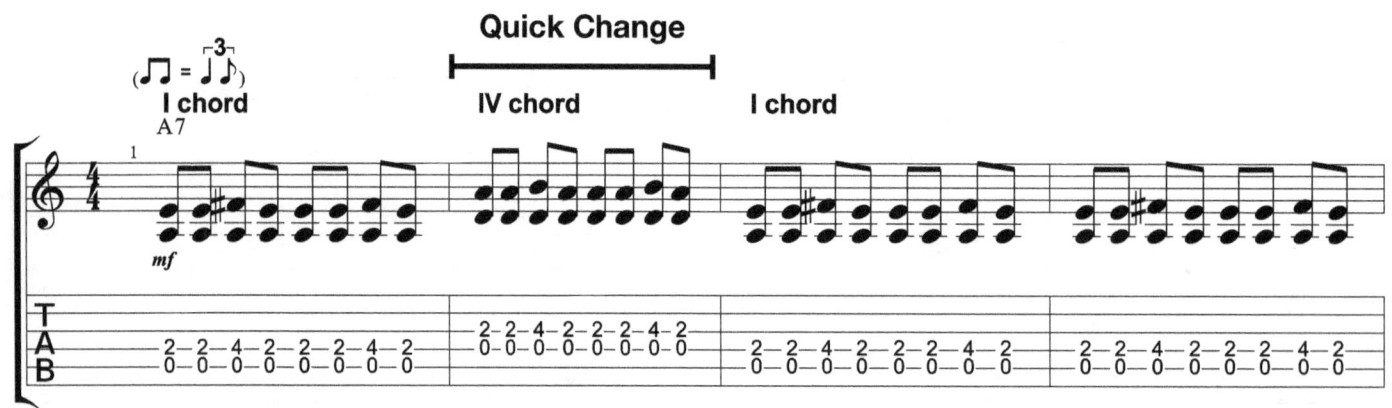

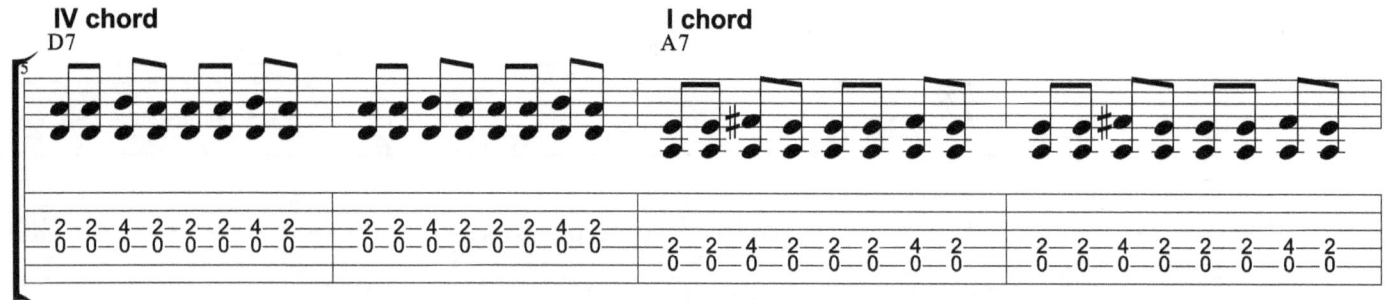

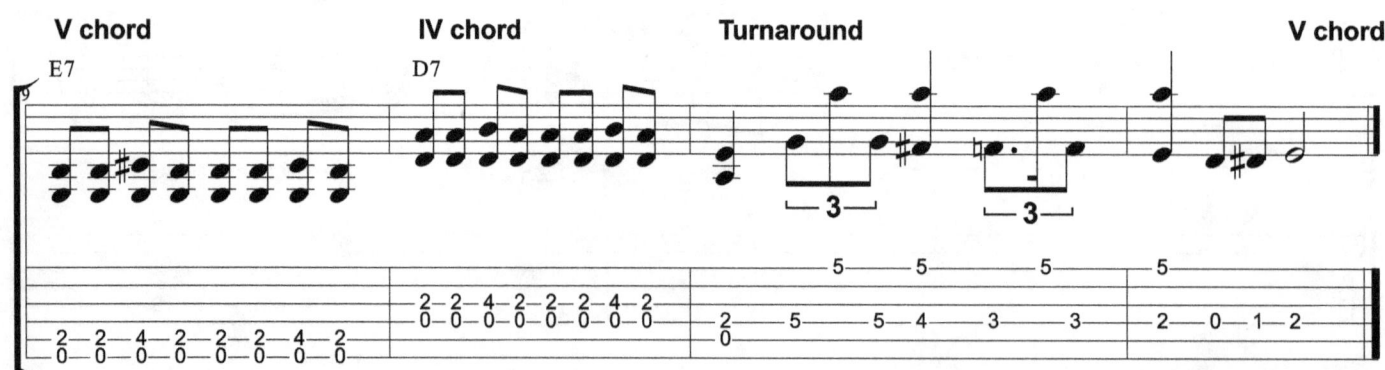

The "Three Phrase" concept for 12 bar blues.

One way that I like to organize a traditional type of 12 bar blues is to think of it as three 4 measure phrases. Not all 12 bar songs are going to be arranged this way but quite a few are and it even helps me play solos that make more sense over the progression, as we will see later on in this book.

We are going to use my song "I'm Gonna Leave" as a example since we have it elsewhere in the book already. First, the lyrics give us our first clue:

Shame on you babe, for thinking lifes' gotta be this way
Shame on you girl, for thinking things' gotta be this way
I'm gonna leave here if you're gonna stay

I'll look at it this way:

Statement: *Shame on you babe, for thinking lifes' gotta be this way*
Re-Statement: *Shame on you girl, for thinking things' gotta be this way*
Punchline or resolution: *I'm gonna leave here if you're gonna stay*

The "statement" happens over the first 4 measure which is predominantly the I chord. The "re-statement" is typically the same lyrical idea but over the IV chord where the melody might change a small amount to fit the new chord. The "punchline" or resolution of what the verse is about is over the last 4 bars and usuallly ends up being a longer or more complex idea.

Within each of these lines there is also a bit of "call and response" though too. "*Shame on you baby*" is the first part and then it resolves with "*for thinking lifes' gotta be this way*". When I solo for one chorus or for the first chorus of a longer solo I will definitely think this way for that first chrous to break things up and to give the solo some structure before moving on to busier or more dynamic ideas. There will be a lesson on that in the second section. For now we are just learning a way to feel the 12 measure form a little easier.

In the example on the next two pages I have both the vocal melody and the guitar part together for you to see how this idea lays out over what you are playing in a Jimmy Reed-style shuffle.

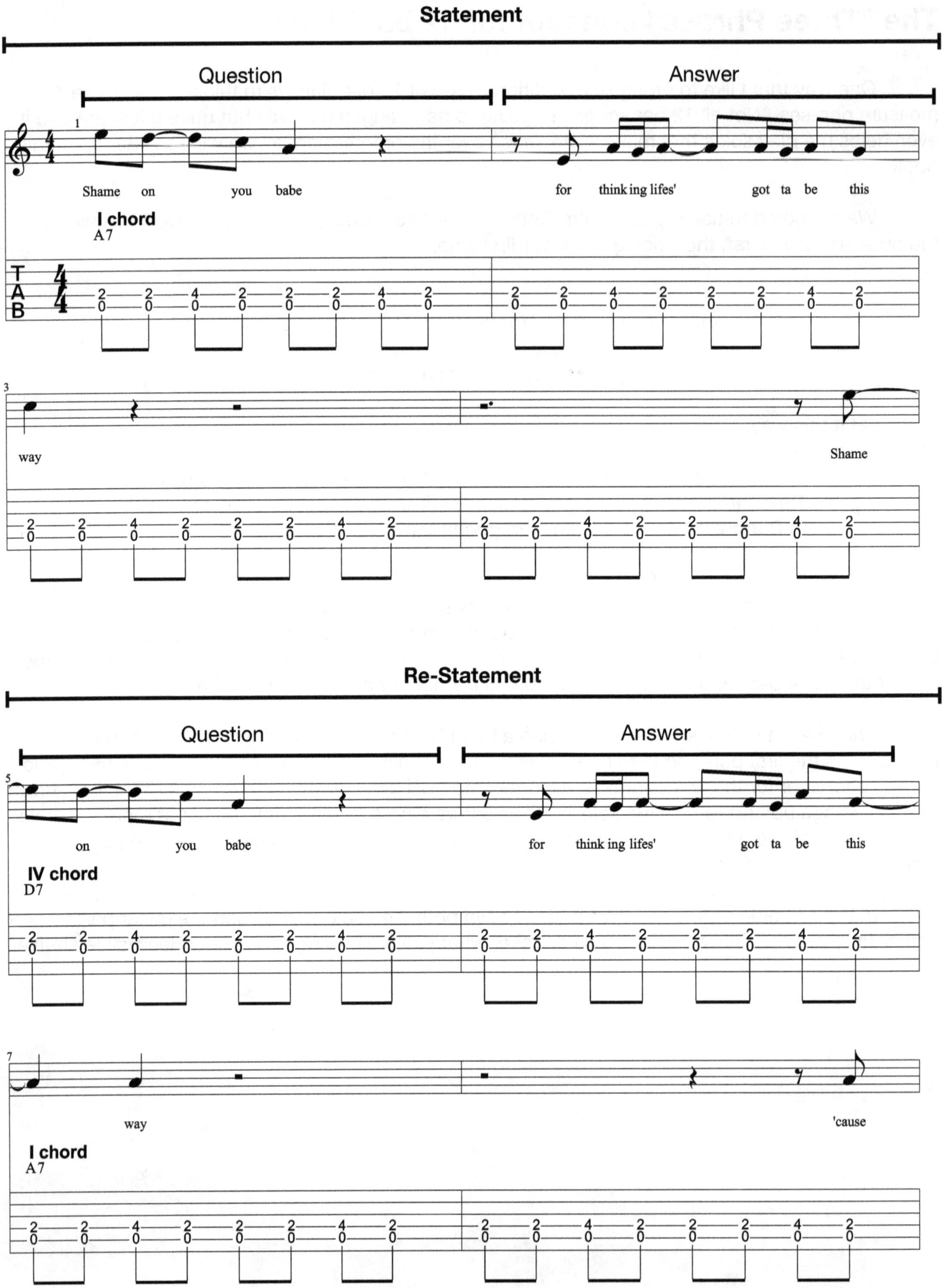

Statement

Question — Shame on you babe [rest] for thinking lifes' got ta be this

I chord
A7

Answer — way [rest] Shame

Re-Statement

Question — on you babe [rest] for thinking lifes' got ta be this

IV chord
D7

Answer — way 'cause

I chord
A7

```
Measures 1–2:
e|--------------------------------|--------------------------------|
B|--2--2--------2--2--2--------2--|--2--2--------2--2--2--------2--|
G|--------4--------------4--------|--------4--------------4--------|
D|--0--0--0--0--0--0--0--0--------|--0--0--0--0--0--0--0--0--------|

Measures 3–4:
B|--2--2--------2--2--2--------2--|--2--2--------2--2--2--------2--|
G|--------4--------------4--------|--------4--------------4--------|
D|--0--0--0--0--0--0--0--0--------|--0--0--0--0--0--0--0--0--------|

Measures 5–6 (D7 / IV chord):
B|--2--2--------2--2--2--------2--|--2--2--------2--2--2--------2--|
G|--------4--------------4--------|--------4--------------4--------|
D|--0--0--0--0--0--0--0--0--------|--0--0--0--0--0--0--0--0--------|

Measures 7–8 (A7 / I chord):
B|--2--2--------2--2--2--------2--|--2--2--------2--2--2--------2--|
G|--------4--------------4--------|--------4--------------4--------|
D|--0--0--0--0--0--0--0--0--------|--0--0--0--0--0--0--0--0--------|
```

The "Three Phrase" concept for 12 bar blues.

One way that I like to organize a traditional type of 12 bar blues is to think of it as three 4 measure phrases. Not all 12 bar songs are going to be arranged this way but quite a few are and it even helps me play solos that make more sense over the progression, as we will see later on in this book.

We are going to use my song "I'm Gonna Leave" as a example since we have it elsewhere in the book already. First, the lyrics give us our first clue:

Shame on you babe, for thinking lifes' gotta be this way
Shame on you girl, for thinking things' gotta be this way
I'm gonna leave here if you're gonna stay

I'll look at it this way:

Statement: *Shame on you babe, for thinking lifes' gotta be this way*
Re-Statement: *Shame on you girl, for thinking things' gotta be this way*
Punchline or resolution: *I'm gonna leave here if you're gonna stay*

The "statement" happens over the first 4 measure which is predominantly the I chord. The "re-statement" is typically the same lyrical idea but over the IV chord where the melody might change a small amount to fit the new chord. The "punchline" or resolution of what the verse is about is over the last 4 bars and usuallly ends up being a longer or more complex idea.

Within each of these lines there is also a bit of "call and response" though too. *"Shame on you baby"* is the first part and then it resolves with "for thinking lifes' gotta be this way". When I solo for one chorus or for the first chorus of a longer solo I will definitely think this way for that first chrous to break things up and to give the solo some structure before moving on to busier or more dynamic ideas. There will be a lesson on that in the second section. For now we are just learning a way to feel the 12 measure form a little easier.

In the example on the next two pages I have both the vocal melody and the guitar part together for you to see how this idea lays out over what you are playing in a Jimmy Reed-style shuffle.

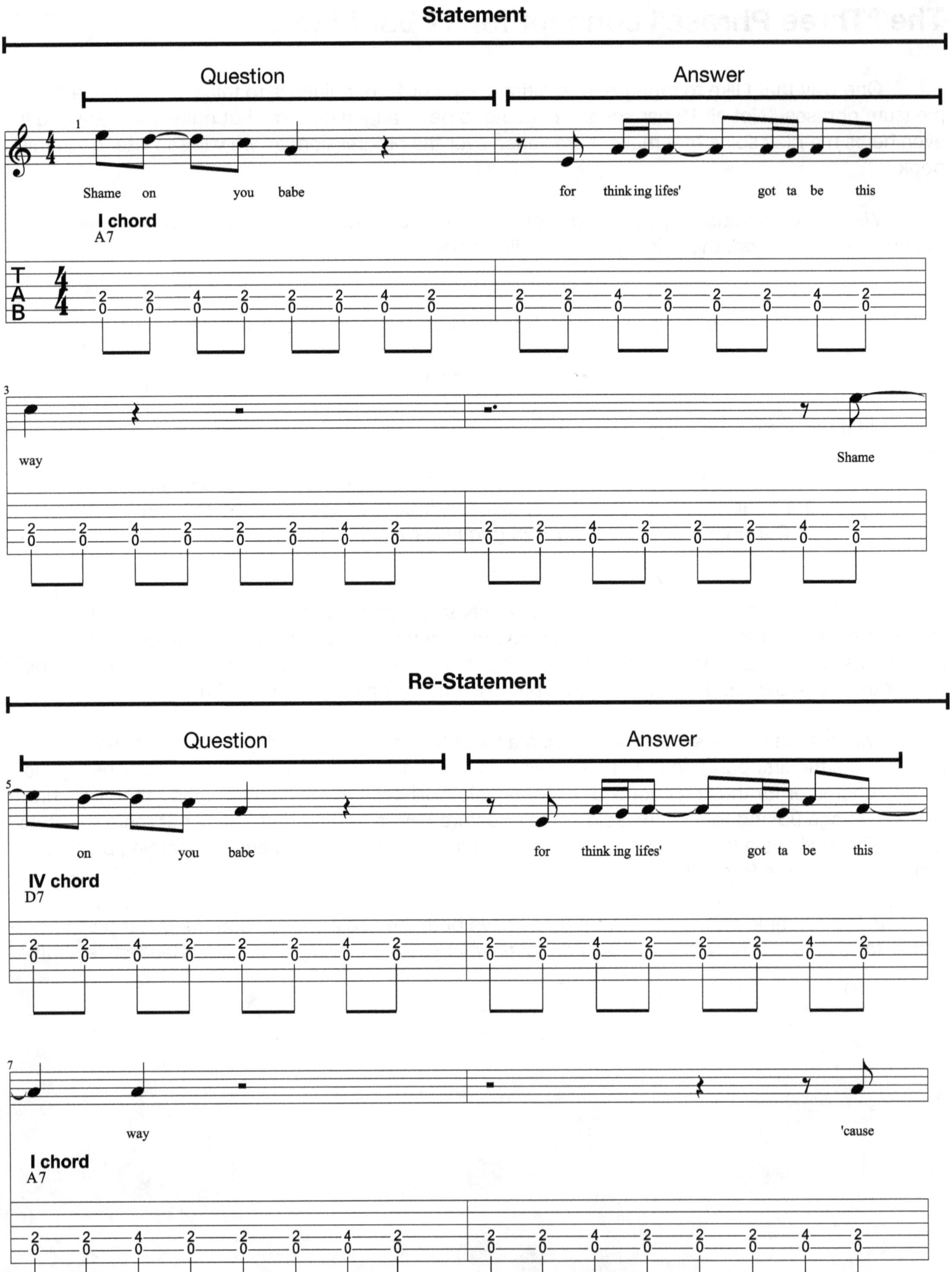

Statement

Question — **Answer**

Shame on you babe / for thinking lifes' got ta be this

I chord
A7

way / Shame

Re-Statement

Question — **Answer**

on you babe / for thinking lifes' got ta be this

IV chord
D7

way / 'cause

I chord
A7

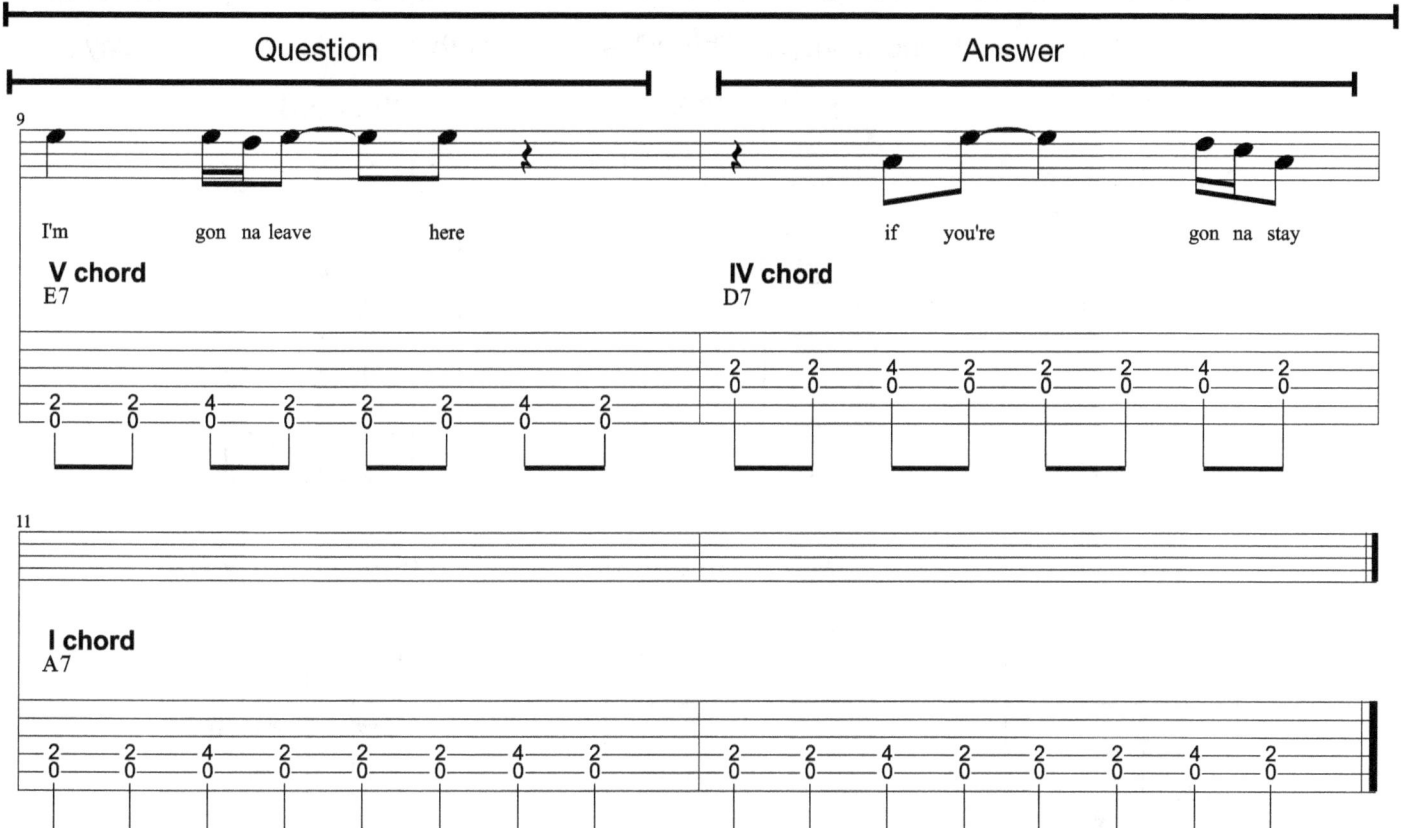

Common Movable Chord Voicings for the upcoming lessons.

The "o" is the root for each chord shape. The "x" is for a root that you don't actually play.

9th chord
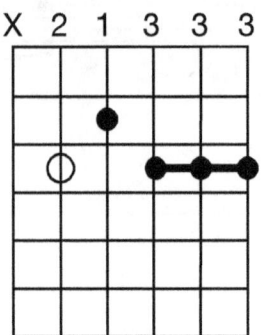

7th chord
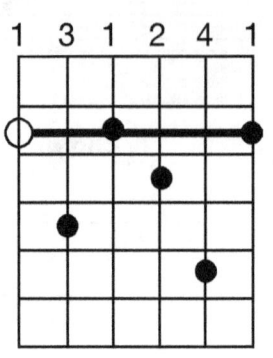

9th chord
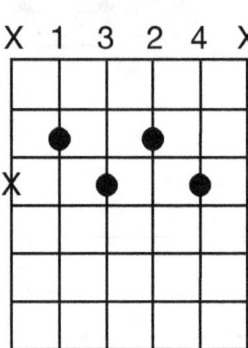

7th chord
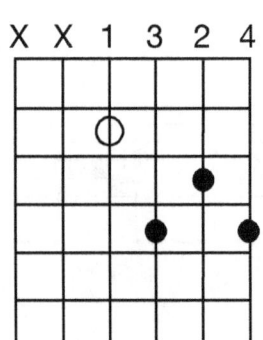

Minor 7th chord
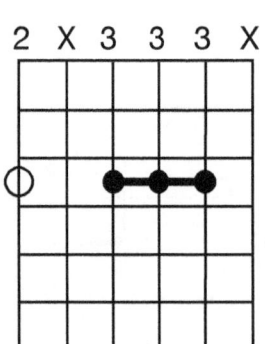

Minor 7th chord
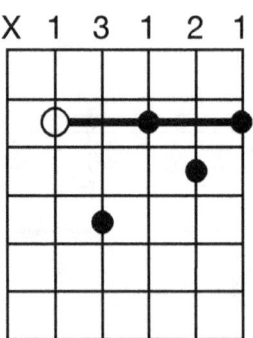

Diminished chord
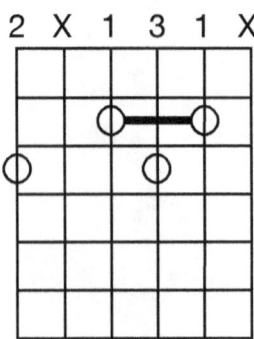

Diminished chord
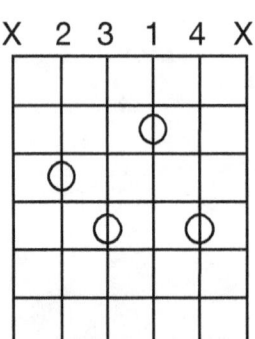

Diminished chord
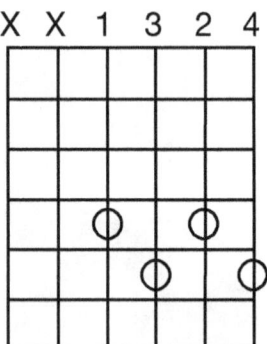

9th chord
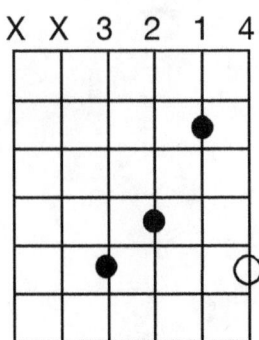

7sus4 chord
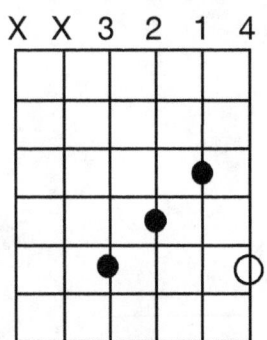

7th chord
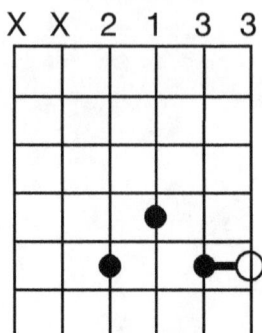

Top and Bottom Parts for a 12 Bar Blues

One incredibly important thing for a guitarist to learn is that there is more to a blues guitar rhythm than the stereotypical Jimmy Reed shuffle. We usually consider a part like that (or any other consistent riff in a lower octave) to be a "bottom" part and if there is more than one guitarist in the band or if you are just looking to change things up you can play a "top" part that is designed to fill in the gaps a bit.

Usually top parts are in an upper octave to stay out of the way of the bottom part and consist of smaller chord voicings or riffs. I have two examples of top parts to share here...one is a very simple upbeat part and the other is more along the lines of what you would hear in a Chicago blues

In this first example I've moved the "Jimmy Reed" part from the other 12 bar blues examples into a closed position...no open strings just to demostrate where else you can play that idea in the key of A. That part is played with all down strokes of the pick. For the "top" part try playing the chords with all up strums since they fall on the "and" or upbeat of each count. Here are the two chord shapes for the top part:

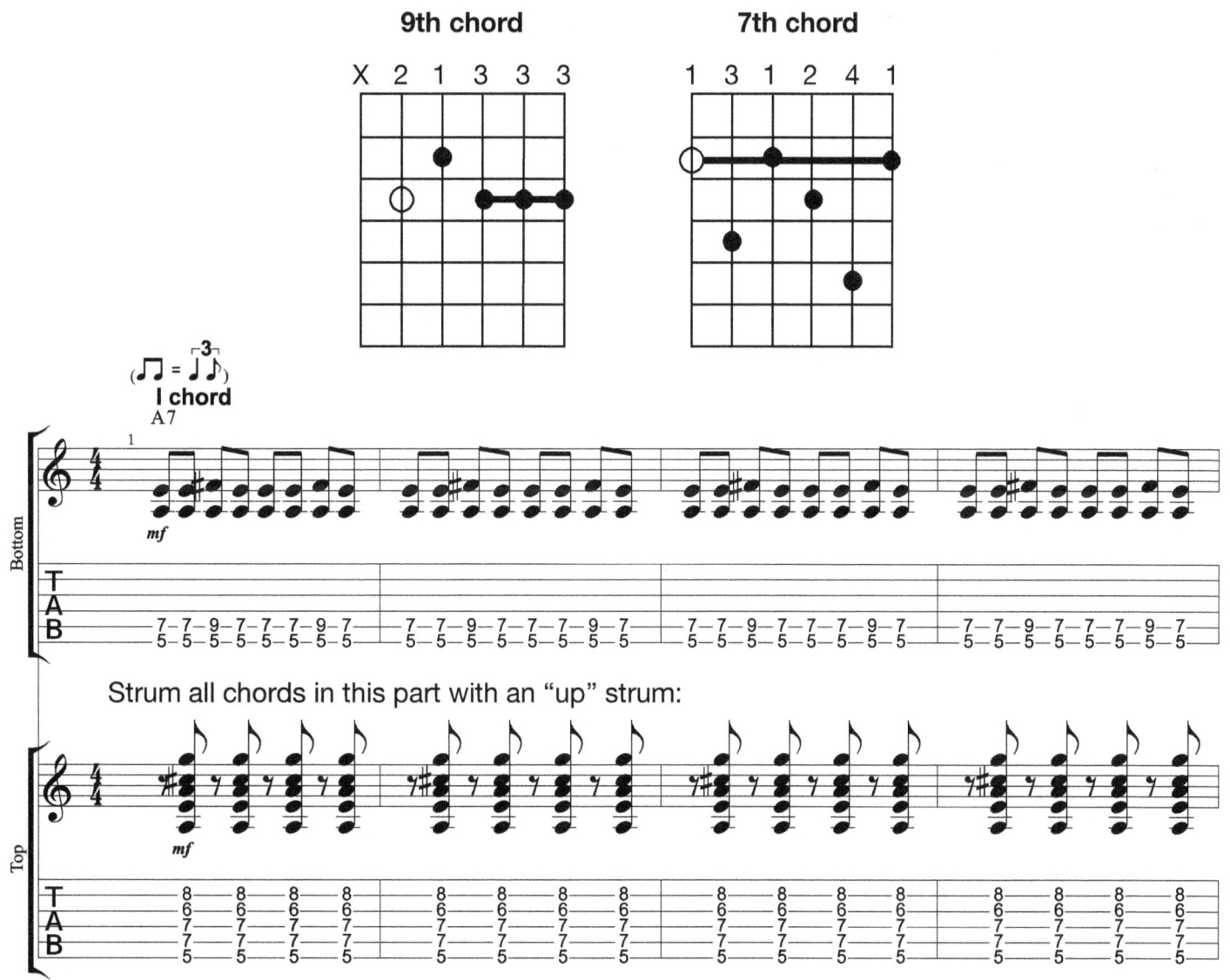

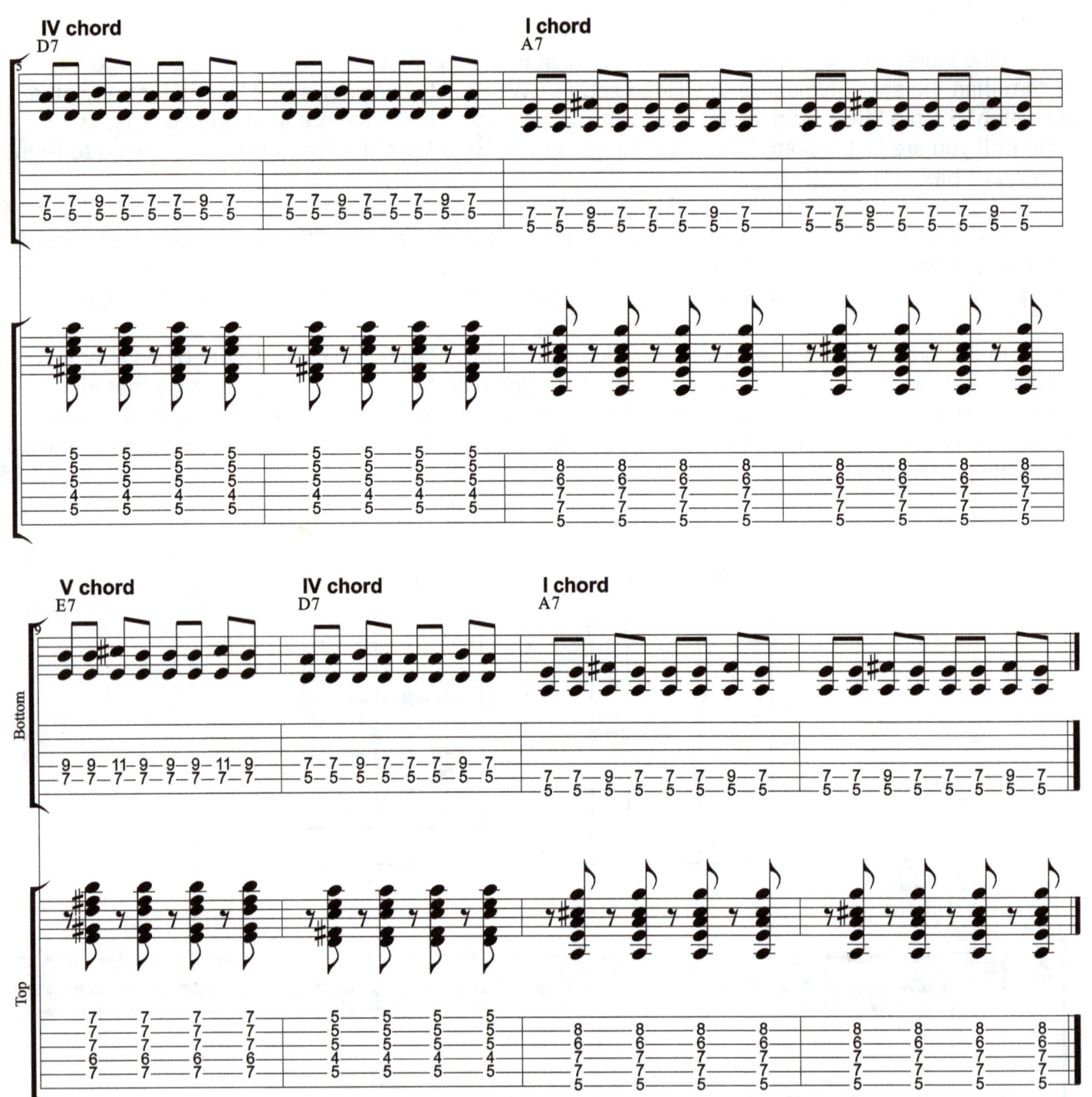

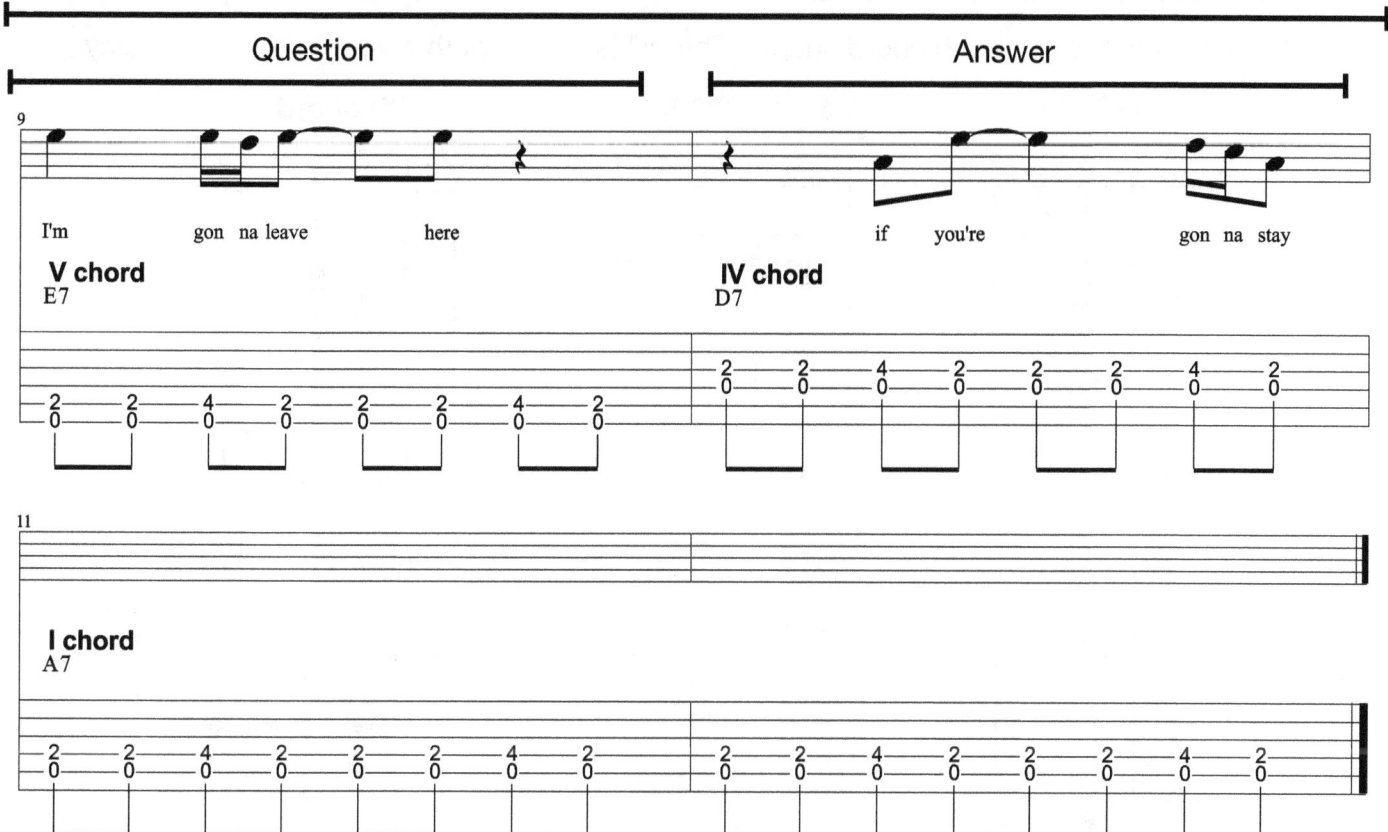

Common Movable Chord Voicings for the upcoming lessons.

The "o" is the root for each chord shape. The "x" is for a root that you don't actually play.

9th chord
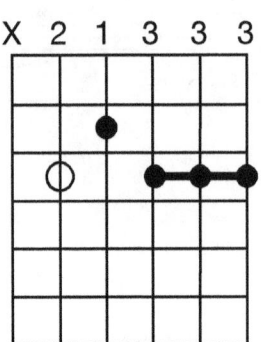

7th chord
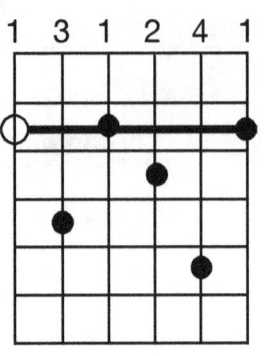

9th chord
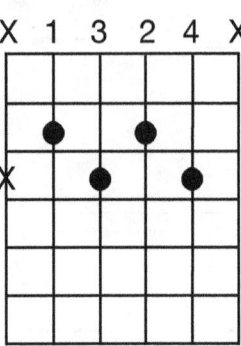

7th chord
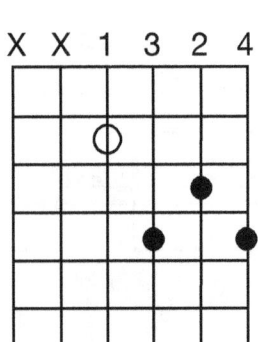

Minor 7th chord
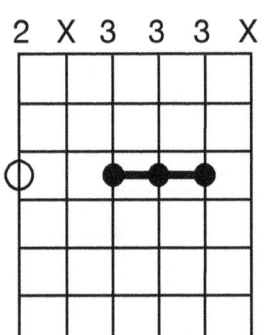

Minor 7th chord
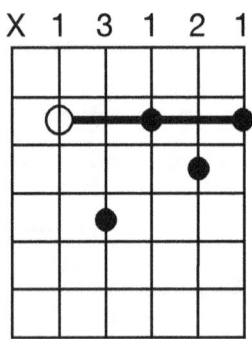

Diminished chord
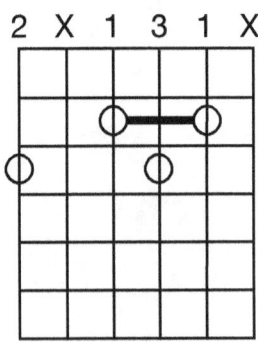

Diminished chord
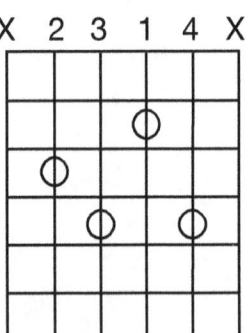

Diminished chord
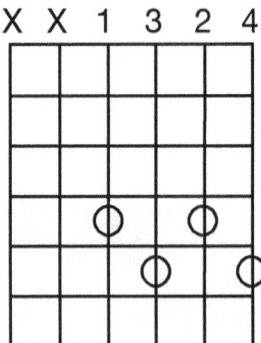

9th chord
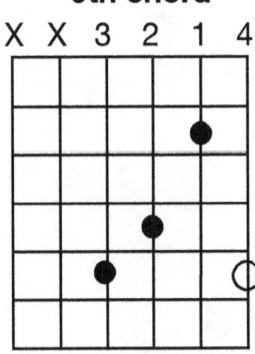

7sus4 chord
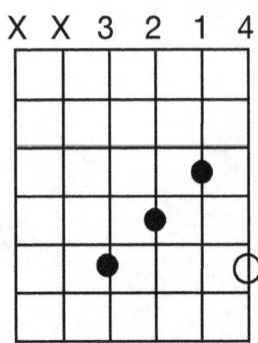

7th chord
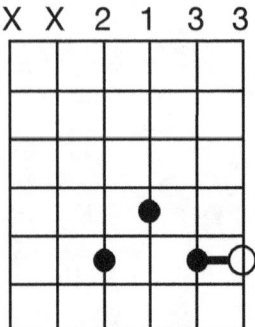

A slighty more complicated top part over the same bottom.

This example utilizes more in the way of 7th and 9th chord fragments and the occasional lick idea. Some of what you see here is similar to the playing you would find by the Meyers brothers or Robert Lockwood Jr when they backed up Little Walter in recordings like "Shake Dancer" or "Key to the Highway". I really like playing this way to fill the space either under or between vocals.

In my song "Someone Elses' Fool" (which is transcribed later in this book) guest guitarist Tommy Harkenrider plays a great top guitar part all the way through the song while I am playing the bottom and singing. I highly suggest learning his top part in that song if you'd like a Master Class in this style of playing. "Someone Elses' Fool" is also an 8 bar blues, so you can see that this fits in a variety of settings. What is important is that you know what chord each lick or idea is played over so that you can move it around in different keys or over different chords in the same chord progression.

Here are two of the chord shapes that make the first four bars interesting by being moved around while keeping a steady triplet rhythm - I love using these ideas to solo with too!

Shape 1 - E7 in the 1st and 3rd measures and E° in the 2nd measure by lowering the whole shape one fret (see tab). The root is not played but you can see I've marked where it would be with the "X" on the 2nd string.

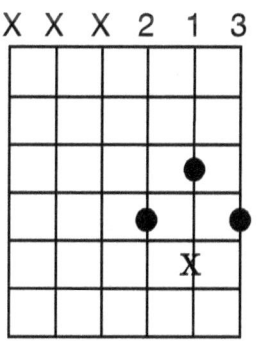

Shape 2 - an E7 voicing that is only played in the 4th measure. Not the most common voicing for this chord and there is no 3rd but its a pretty cool sound!

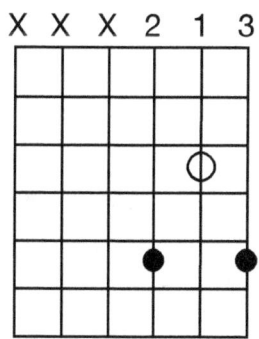

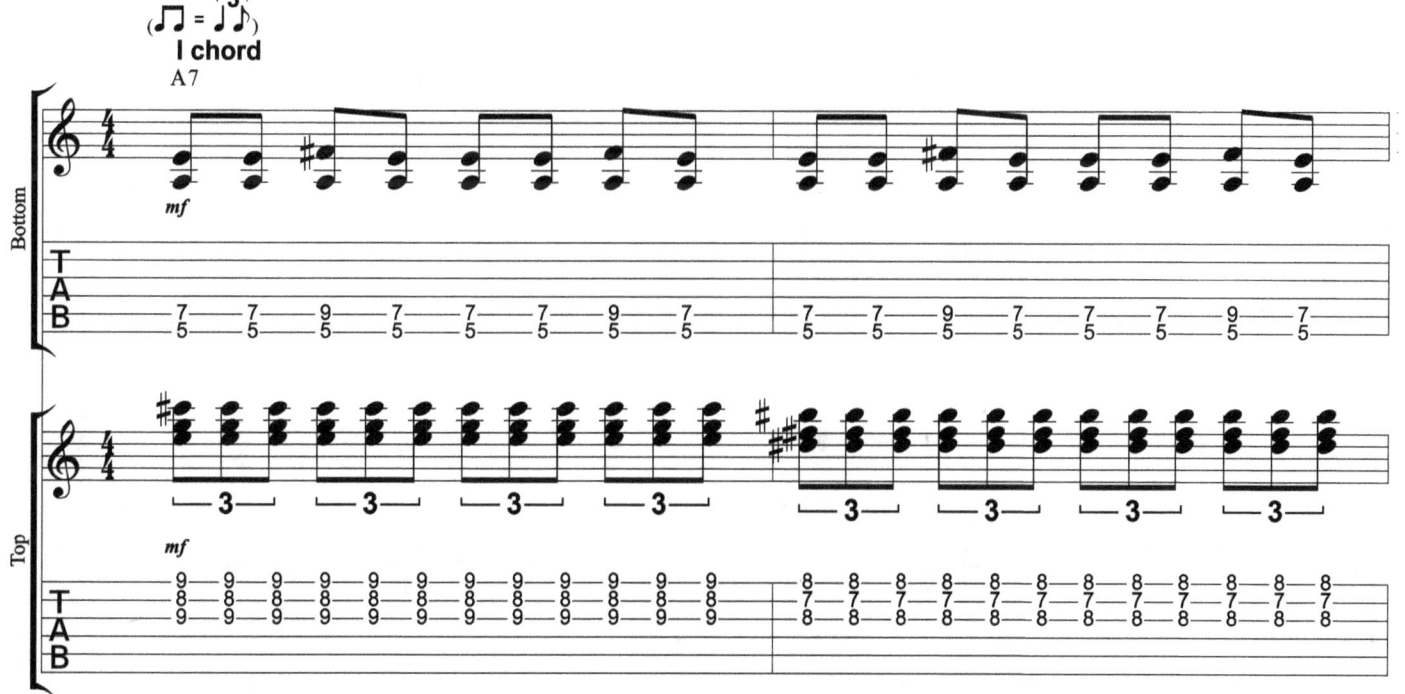

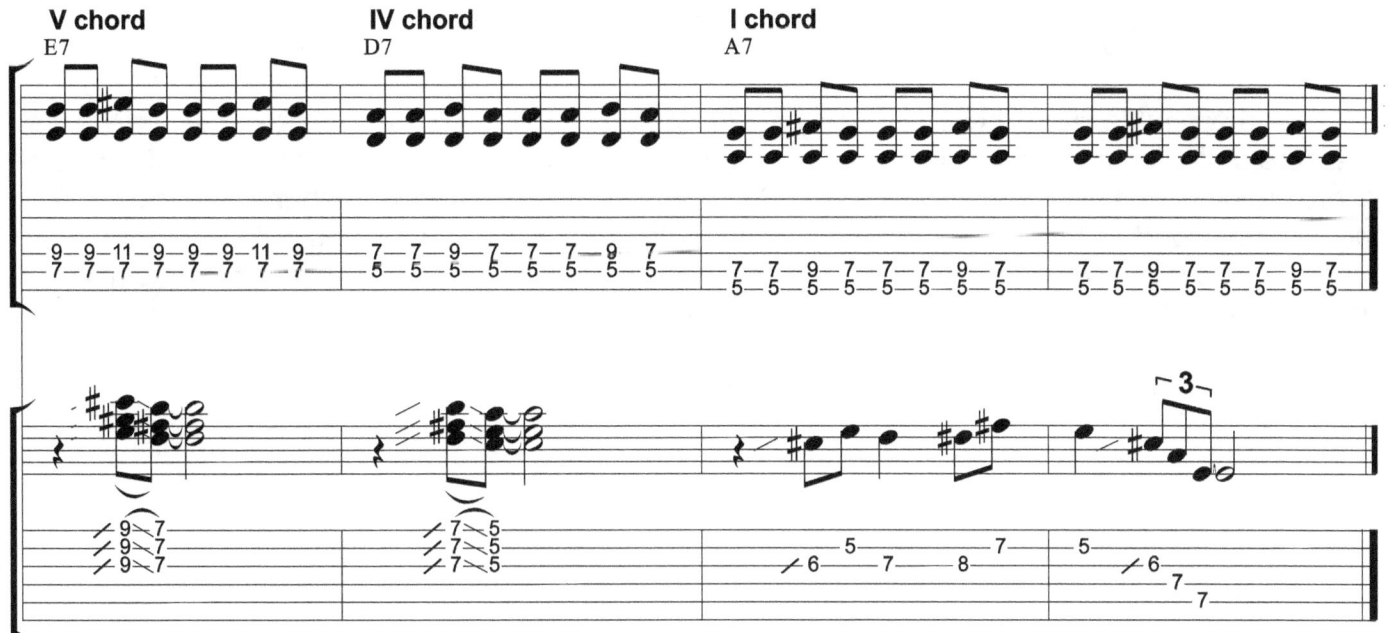

Sliding 9ths!

The sliding chord fragments in 5th and 6th and 9th and 10th measure in this example are a pretty common idea that is derived from this 9th chord shape.

The three notes that you play with a partial barre on the first three strings are the part that you are sliding around but as long as you keep track of where the root is in the chord voicing you should be able to move the idea around into any key!

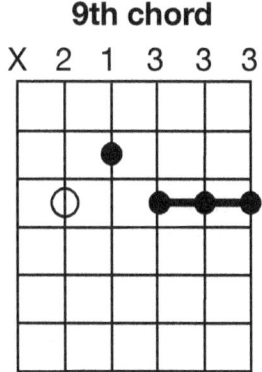

This 9th chord voicing does not have a root that you play. The "X" that I've placed on the 6th string shows you where the root actually is. We typically use this chord when there is a full band playing and the bassist is most likely playing a root in his part. When we do the chord slides below we do not move the 1st finger with the rest of the chord.

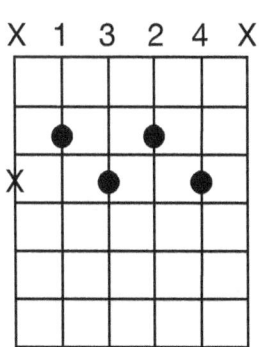

Box Shuffles

A box shuffle is another way to play a 12 bar blues. The box pattern that you see in the first measure of the example below is a one measure riff that you move around just like any of your other chord shapes. The first note in this case is the root. I've added a second part in case you are playing with a second guitarist so that you have something to play that keeps you out of the way of the main riff (which is also usually what the bassist is doing) and fills out the groove. Remember that we have full versions of both types of box shuffle with backing tracks on the website.

Here is a variation on the box shuffle pattern above. We will call it a reverse box pattern and it is used the same way as the previous example. The second guitar part is a little different as well. This time we are sliding fragments of 9th chords around, similar to how we did it in the more advanced top part for the 12 bar top and bottom example. The one difference is that we now have a 9th chord with the root on the 6th string so we don't have to move around on the fretboard quite so much.

The Boogaloo

This is another box-type feel for a 12 bar blues. I have never been sure where the Boogaloo name comes from since if you listen to authentic Latin American Boogaloo music from the 1960's it doesn't sound much like this. The same goes for the Latin or "Mambo" blues, but these are the names that we know these feels by, so thats what we have.

In this case we are using a similar box pattern but the big difference is that we have a straight eighth note feel and not a shuffle. The second guitar part is more of a backbeat or "stab" part with small chords on beat 2 of each measure and every 4 bars I have a little slide embellishment. "Messing with the Kid" by Junior Wells is a good example of this sort of feel.

For the Boogaloo and the Mambo on the next page I am just giving you examples of the riff or rhythmic figure for each feel. Move them around just like you would any of your moveable chord shapes or scales to play a full 12 bar blues with the ideas. You have the I and IV chords in the key of A written out. Just move the IV riff up two frets for your V chord! See website for full version.

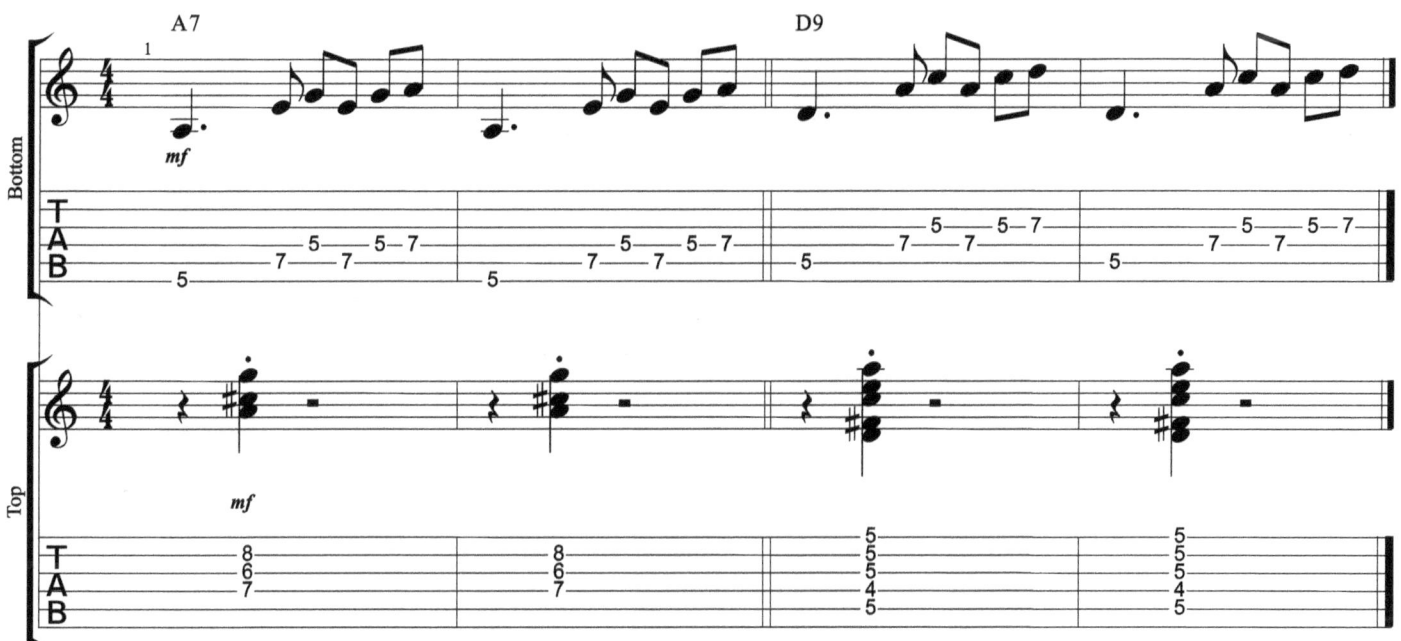

29

Latin Blues or the "Blues Mambo"

This is another of the Latin-influenced feels that is good for you to be familiar with. "Crosscut Saw" by Albert King is probably my favorite example of this one. The bottom part is similar to the Boogaloo although the Mambo bass line includes the third and sixth chord tones which gives it more of a major sound as opposed to the Boogaloo, which has a minor 7th and no 3rd.

The top part in this example is actually a mishmash of parts that I could play. The first 2 bars have one kind of picking pattern and the IV has another. Definitely experiment with the two variations shown in this part and see which one you like better. See website for full version.

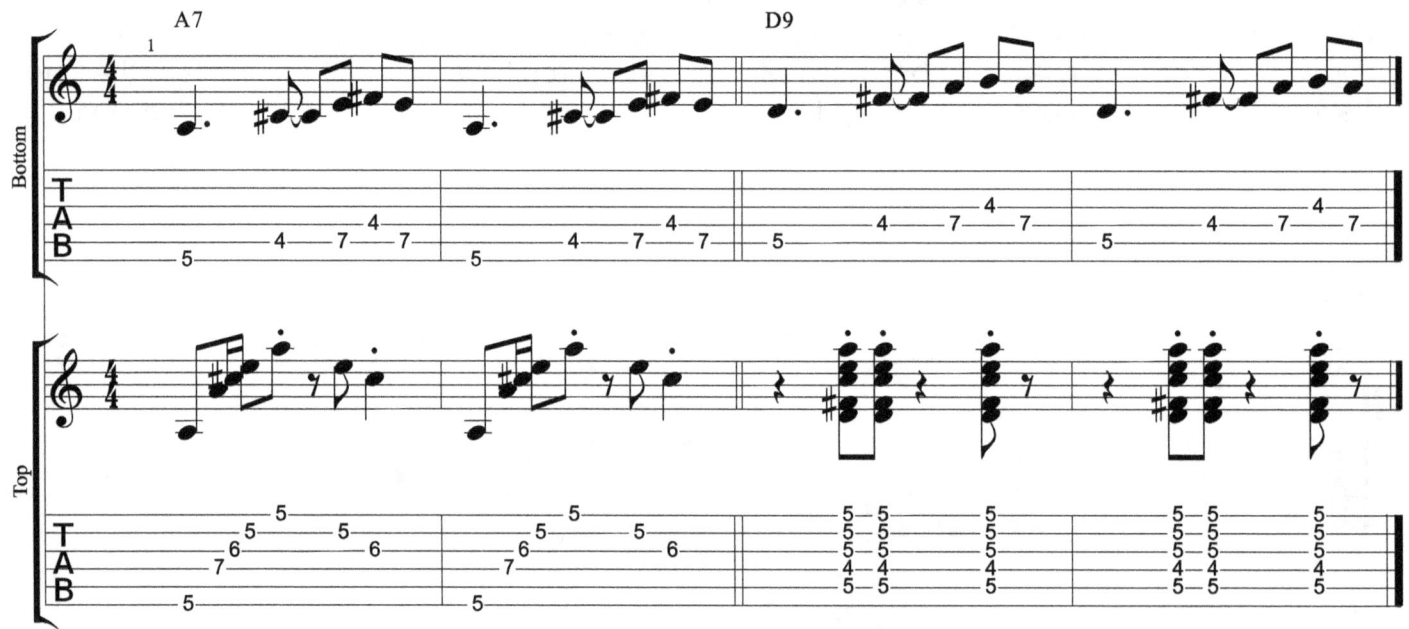

Eight Bar Blues

The eight bar blues is a little less common than the 12 bar blues progression but it is still important to know. As stated in the name it is eight measures in length, and comes in a couple of different varieties.

My personal favorite is the version that is used in the song "It Hurts Me Too" that artists such as Elmore James and Junior Wells have made popular. I also use it in my song "Someone Else's Fool", which is transcribed later in this book.

Variation 1:

I chord for 2 measures

IV chord for 2 measures

I chord for 1 measure

V chord for 1 measure

I chord for 2 measures

The last two measures almost always consist of a turnaround in any of these 8 bar blues forms.

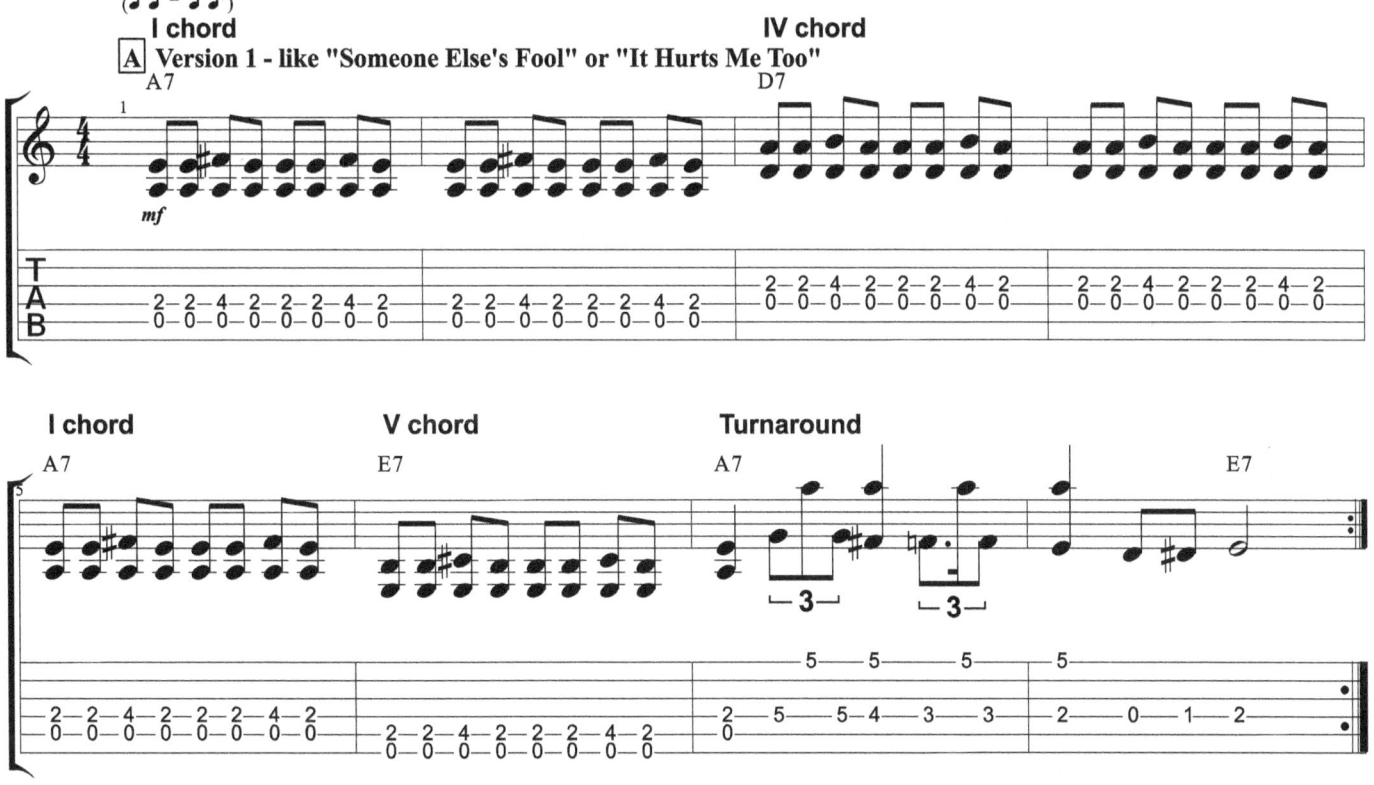

The second variation is more like the progression for "Key to the Highway". It is a more popular song due to versions by Eric Clapton, Freddy King, Little Walter and a ton of other artists but I'm not aware of many other songs that use this progression:

Variation 2:

I chord for 1 measures

V chord for 1 measure

IV chord for 2 measures

I chord for 1 measure

V chord for 1 measure

I chord for two measures

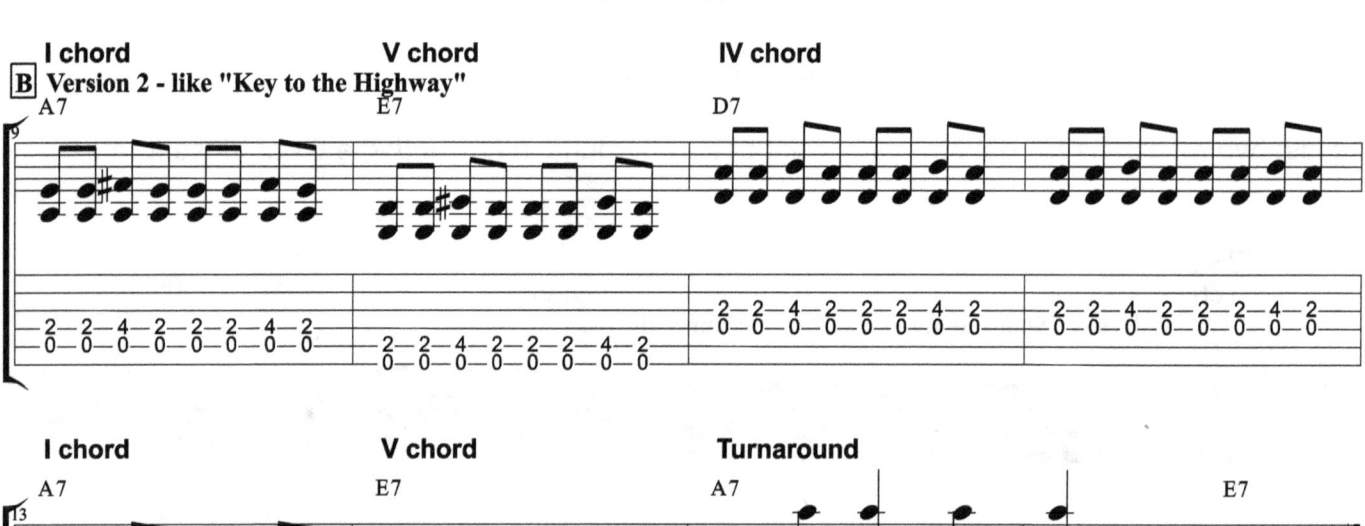

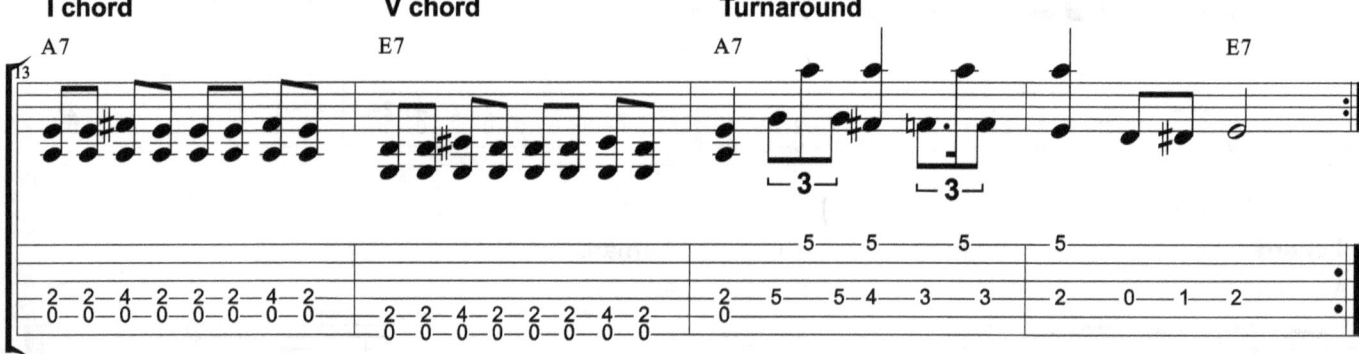

Minor Blues

A Minor Blues chord progression is usually also a 12 measure form but there are many variations on what chords can be in a minor blues progression.

A good starting point is to just make all of the chords that naturally occur in a standard 12 bar blues minor chords:

i chord for 4 measures

iv chord for 2 measures

i chord for 2 measures

v chord for one measure

iv chord for one measure

i chord for two measures

Notice that I am using the lower case roman numerals for these chords to indicate that they are minor chords.

Since the standard "Jimmy Reed" riff does not work for a minor blues as it does in the 12 and 8 bar forms we are just playing some simple minor seventh chords to hear the harmony. As we explore the different feels you can apply to these chord progressions I will give you some options for rhythm parts that will work over a minor blues. For now just play the chords as written and count the measures to get a feel for how these variations on the minor blues sound. And honestly there are many variations...these are just a few of the more common ones you might run across.

A couple of chord voicings you can try out as you play through the examples:

Minor 7th chord   **Minor 7th chord**

2 X 3 3 3 X   X 1 3 1 2 1

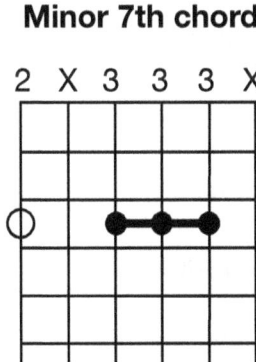 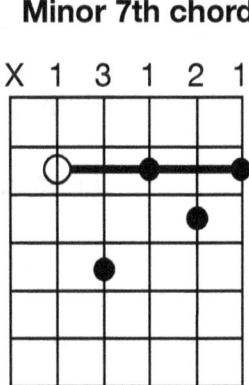

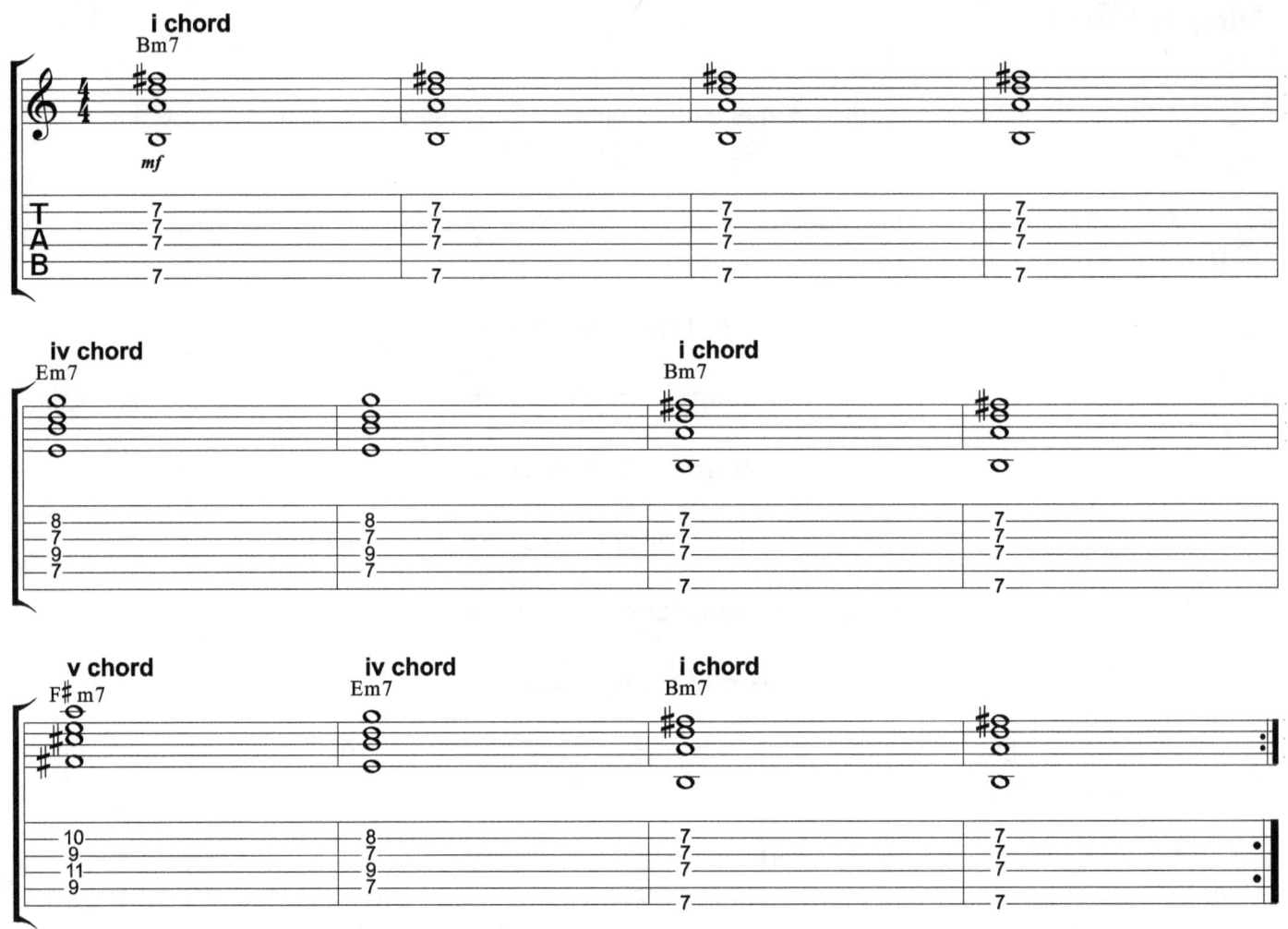

Sometimes we can substitute some major or dominant chords in for the iv and v chords. In my song "Subterrania (The Prize)" (which is transcribed later in this book) I use a dominant IV chord in the 5th and 6th measures but return to the minor iv chord in the 10th measure:

i chord for 4 measures

IV chord for 2 measures

i chord for 2 measures

v chord for one measure

iv chord for one measure

i chord for two measures

Another well known example of this is "The Thrill is Gone" as popularized by B.B. King:

i chord for 4 measures

IV chord for 2 measures

i chord for 2 measures

bVI chord for one measure

V chord for one measure

i chord for two measures

In that song we have a bVI ("flat six") chord in the ninth bar and a major or dominant V chord in the 10th bar. Its a very strong sound that is pretty fun to play over if you can target some of the chord tones of those chords.

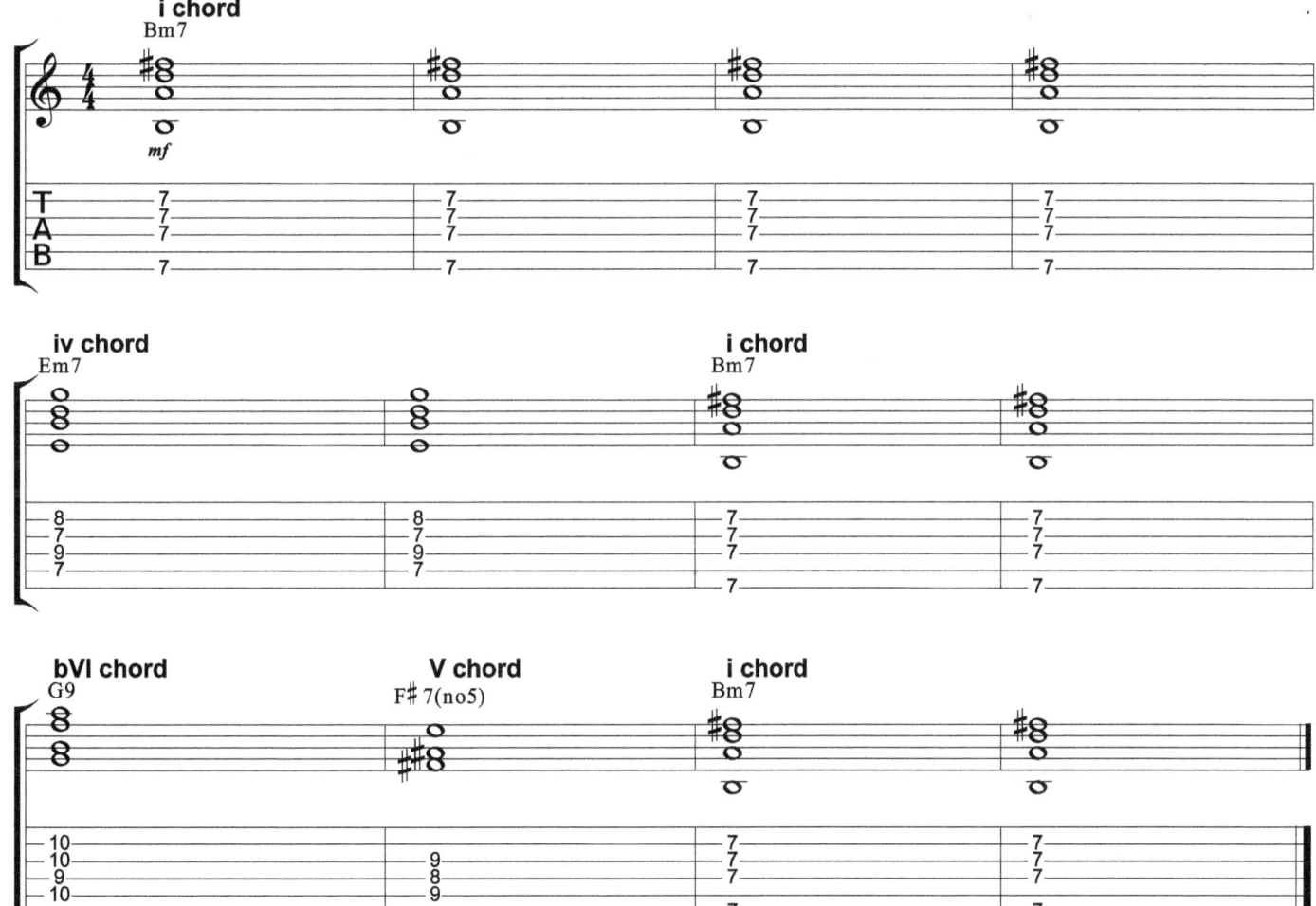

35

Section 2

• • •

Glossary of Scales and other Theory

Minor Blues

A Minor Blues chord progression is usually also a 12 measure form but there are many variations on what chords can be in a minor blues progression.

A good starting point is to just make all of the chords that naturally occur in a standard 12 bar blues minor chords:

i chord for 4 measures

iv chord for 2 measures

i chord for 2 measures

v chord for one measure

iv chord for one measure

i chord for two measures

Notice that I am using the lower case roman numerals for these chords to indicate that they are minor chords.

Since the standard "Jimmy Reed" riff does not work for a minor blues as it does in the 12 and 8 bar forms we are just playing some simple minor seventh chords to hear the harmony. As we explore the different feels you can apply to these chord progressions I will give you some options for rhythm parts that will work over a minor blues. For now just play the chords as written and count the measures to get a feel for how these variations on the minor blues sound. And honestly there are many variations...these are just a few of the more common ones you might run across.

A couple of chord voicings you can try out as you play through the examples:

Minor 7th chord

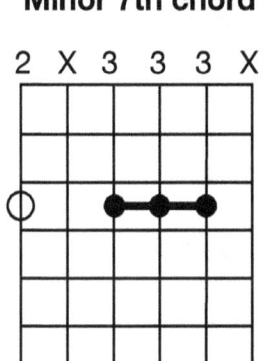

Minor 7th chord

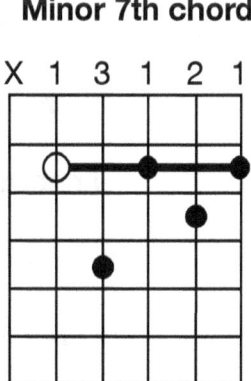

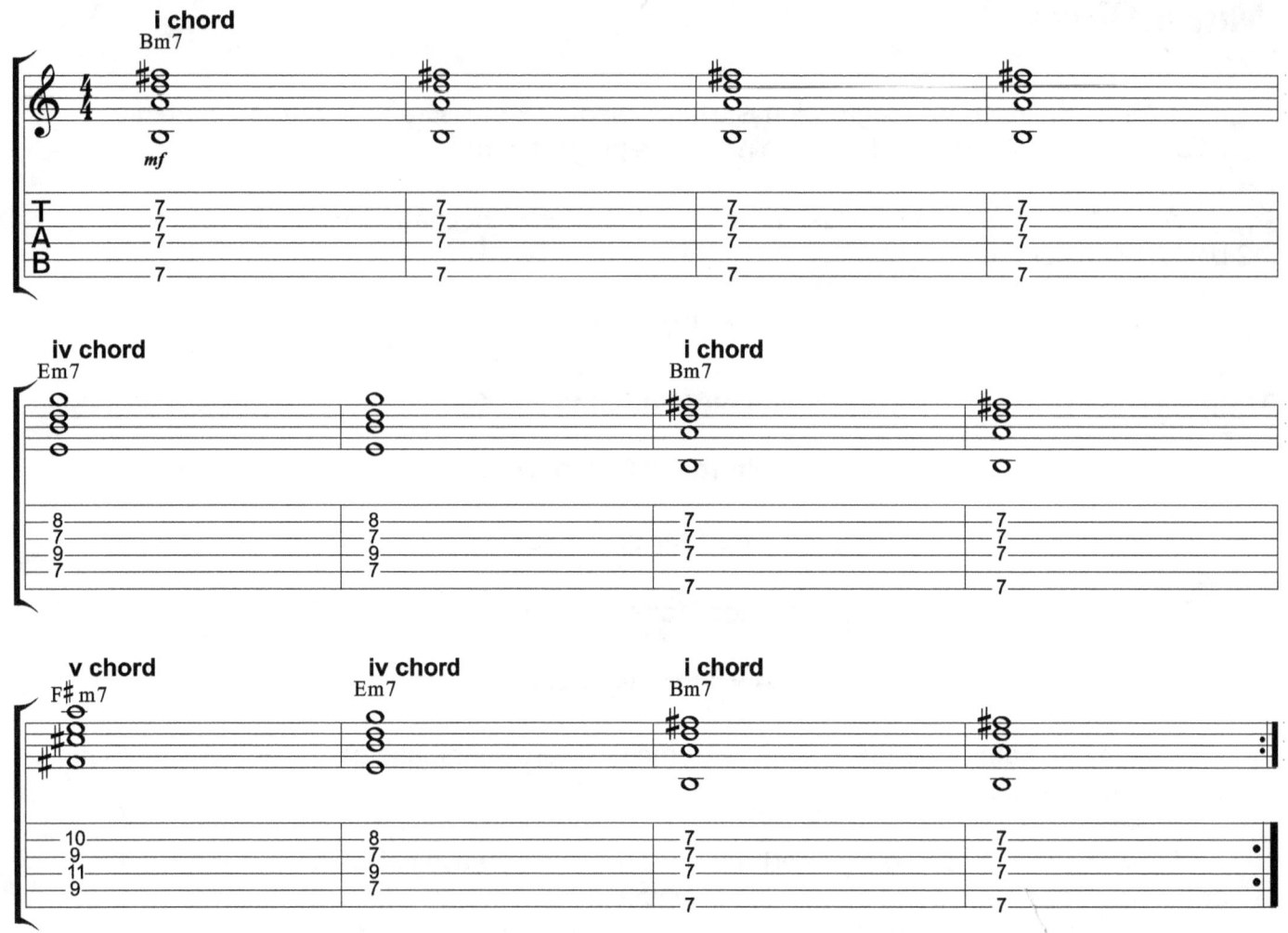

Sometimes we can substitute some major or dominant chords in for the iv and v chords. In my song "Subterrania (The Prize)" (which is transcribed later in this book) I use a dominant IV chord in the 5th and 6th measures but return to the minor iv chord in the 10th measure:

i chord for 4 measures

IV chord for 2 measures

i chord for 2 measures

v chord for one measure

iv chord for one measure

i chord for two measures

How I am presenting the lead guitar material in this book:

This isn't a music theory book by any stretch of the imagination and I am assuming that you already play guitar to some point so you should understand some basics about how to read chord and neck diagrams and tablature. This section is largely a reference for scales and arpeggios that I will use later in the book How I'm going to present this information is a little different than what you might be used to so I want to discuss that here before we dive in.

The numbers that you see on the diagram below are called "scale degrees", which are the names that we are going to call each note in the scale. I want to give you a way of understanding what these scales are that will allow you to use them much more intuitively than if they were just a bunch of dots on a fretboard. And if you just want to learn the scale patterns and not worry about what the numbers mean that is OK too, but this is how I like to teach and it seems to be pretty effective with my students when we work on fretboard theory.

Using the numbers instead of dots on the fretboard for where you put your fingers will hopefully show you how to start seeing where ideas can be and *are* repeated in the scale. Remember that there are only 5 notes in a pentatonic scale and one added to that for a blues scale (the b5). The amount of repetition that happens is huge in an average solo and if you start seeing the scales this way you'll also start being able to move your own licks around.

First of all, the numbers. They are what we discussed in the very beginning of this book when we talked about chord progressions. A minor or Blues scale will have different relative distances between notes to make their sounds though so we need to alter this a bit.

Major Scale Notes	C	D	E	F	G	A	B
Major Scale Degrees	1	2	3	4	5	6	7
Minor Scale Notes	C	D	Eb	F	G	Ab	Bb
Minor Scale Degrees	1	2	minor 3	4	5	minor 6	minor 7
Minor Pentatonic Notes	C		Eb	F	G		Bb
Minor Pentatonic Degrees	C		minor 3	4	5		minor 7

If a scale degree is "minor" it means that you are lowering the note one half step or one fret on the guitar. For our scale patterns below a minor 3rd is written as "m3". If you notice above the Minor pentatonic scale is the same as the Minor scale except that we have removed the 2nd and 6th notes. For a "Blues Scale" we add the "diminished 5" between the 4 and the 5. I'm also replacing the "1" with an "R" for "Root" since that is also the root of the scale and any chords that we'll be building from this.

C Blues Scale

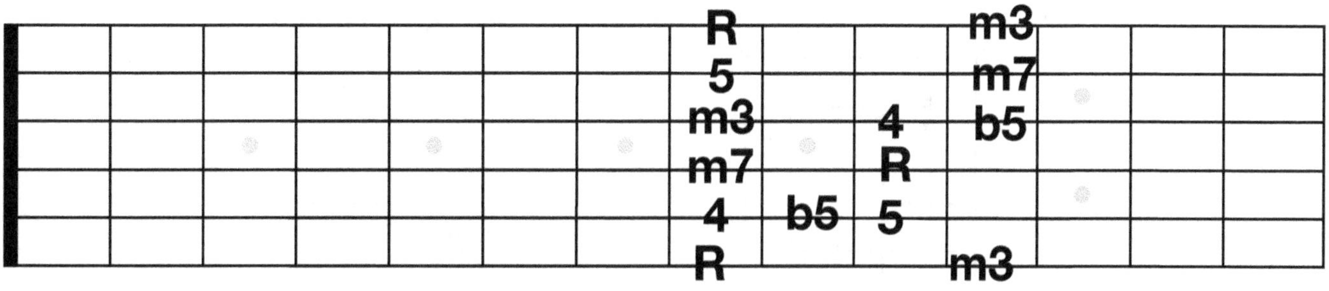

						R			m3			
						5			m7			
						m3		4	b5			
						m7		R				
						4	b5	5				
						R			m3			

37

If you want to use this scale in another key then move the whole pattern down until the root of the pattern is on the root of the key you want. The blues scale on the previous page is in the key of C since the root is on the C on the 8th fret 6th string. The scales on the next page have been moved into other positions to fit them into the guitar necks. They are NOT all in the same key.

The CAGED System

This is a system of organizing your fretboard into smaller sections based off of your open chords. The first thing that we will do is to take the root of each chord out of the shapes for your open C, open A, open G, open E and open D shapes (the so-called "campfire chords" that most of us learn when first pick up a guitar). It is a great place to start but you definitely want to start connecting these patterns into one larger neck pattern sooner rather than later so that you have a more complete ability to play anywhere in any key on the guitar.

The open dots are the roots for each chord. You'll notice that for the A, G, E and D chords there are roots that fall on open strings and the "o" for a root is larger than the "0" for the normal open string fingering indication. On the next page we have the root patterns written out horizontally on guitar necks for you to see how they all lay out to play a C# note all over the fretboard. If you play the patterns in order they spell out the word "CAGED" with their chord names. You'll also see that every note is part of two root shapes...one above it and one below it on the fretboard.

Once you are comfortable with these shapes we can move on to learning each of the scales that I use on a fairly regular basis to play this music. Not every sound is in this book but these will get you through most blues, rock and soul playing situations.

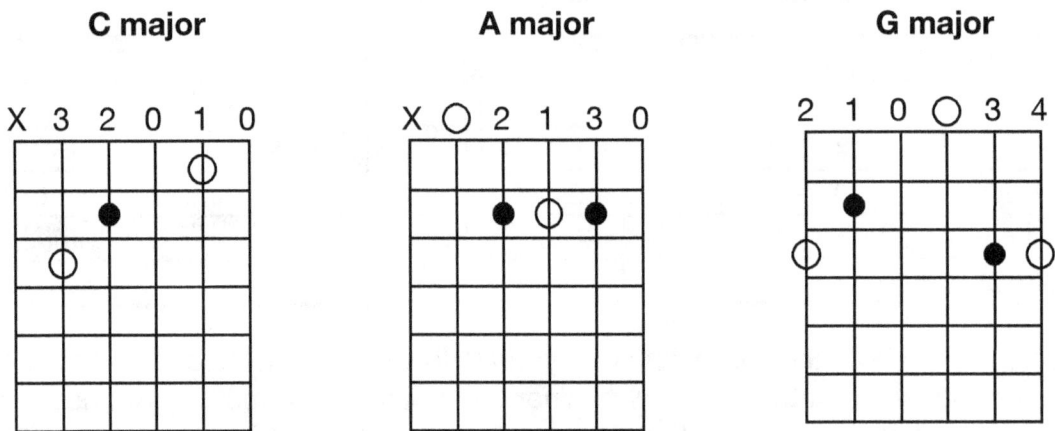

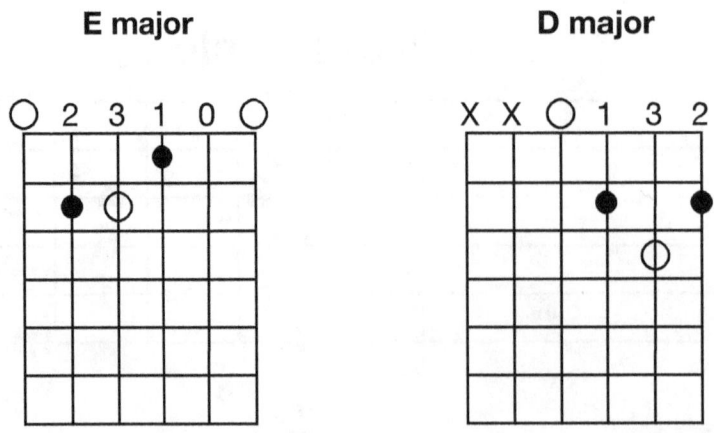

38

Root Patterns from the CAGED System

C Major Shape

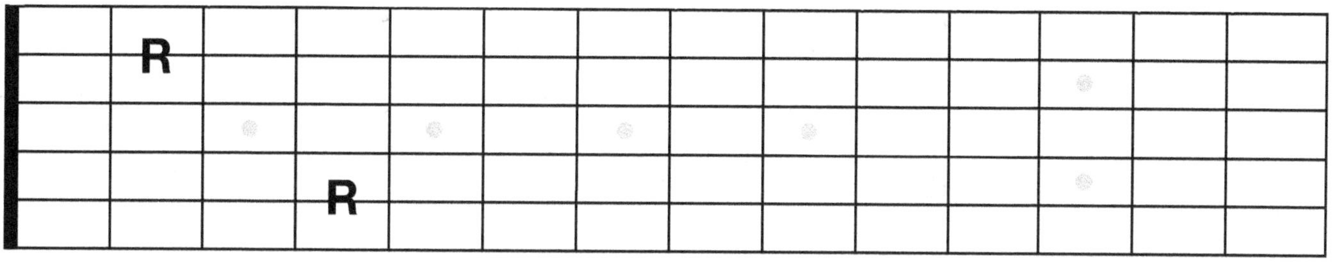

A Major Shape

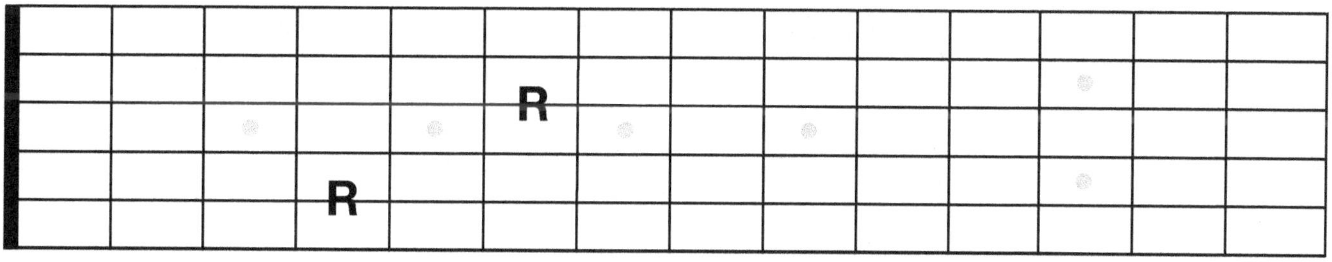

G Major Shape

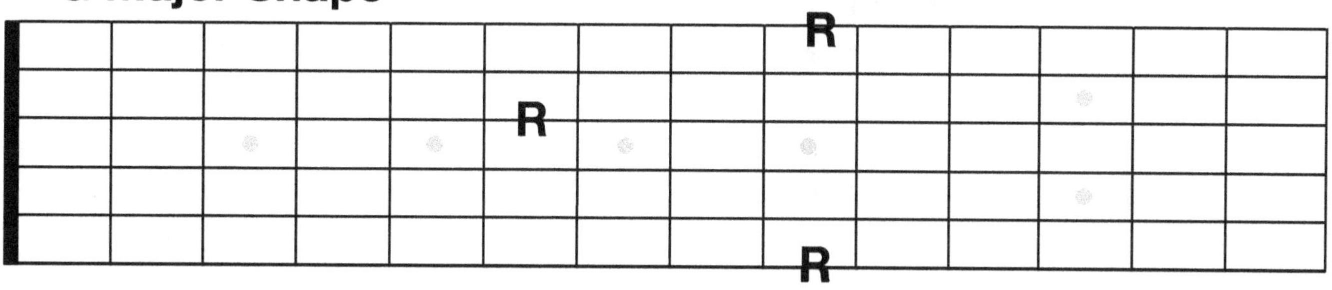

E Major Shape

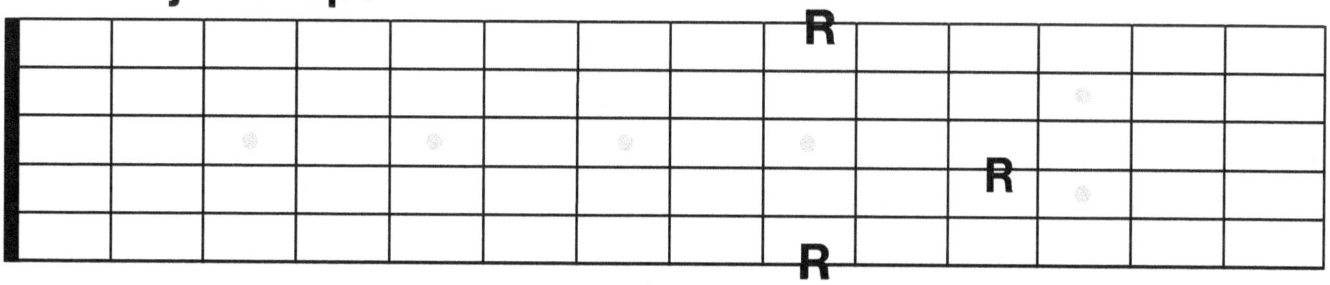

D Major Shape

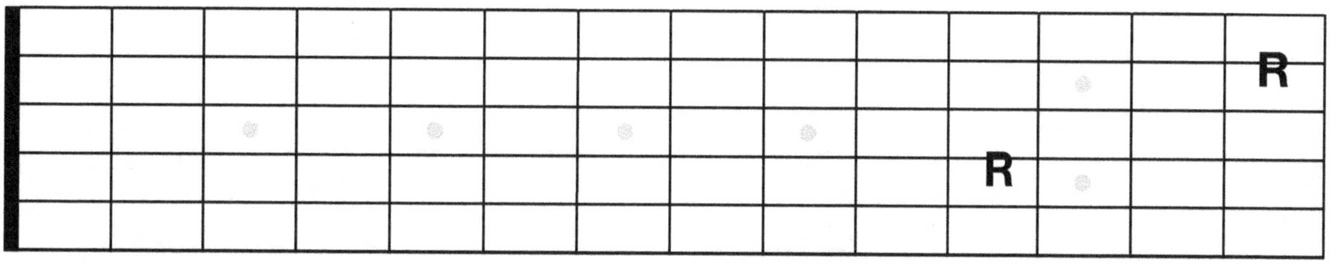

Minor Pentatonic

E Shape

D Shape

C Shape

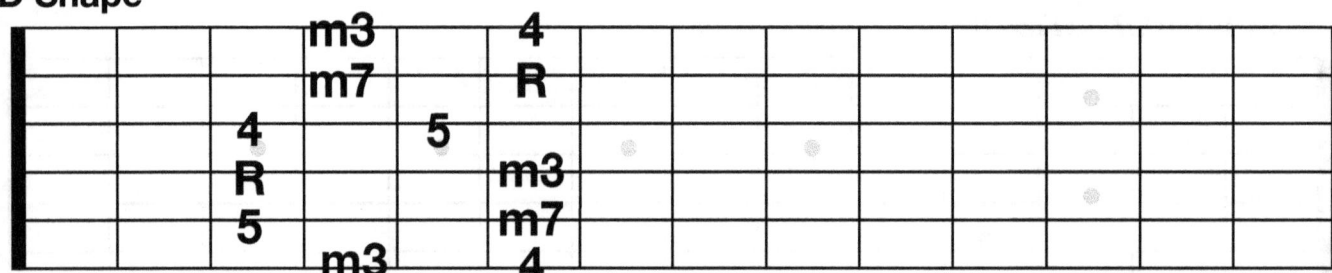

A Shape

G Shape

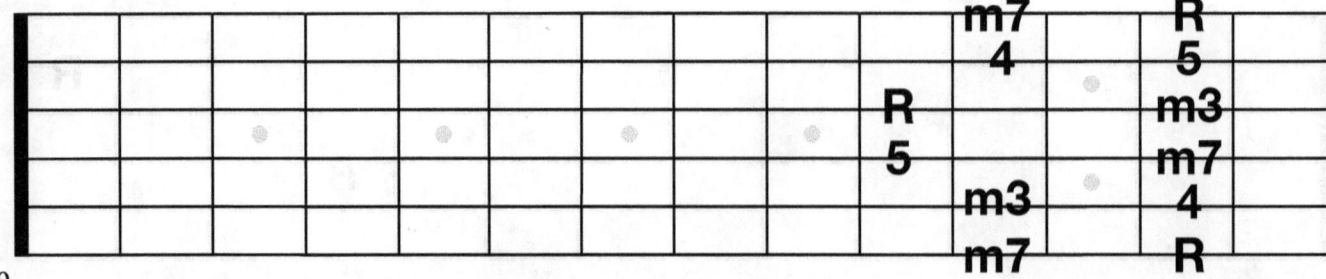

How I am presenting the lead guitar material in this book:

This isn't a music theory book by any stretch of the imagination and I am assuming that you already play guitar to some point so you should understand some basics about how to read chord and neck diagrams and tablature. This section is largely a reference for scales and arpeggios that I will use later in the book How I'm going to present this information is a little different than what you might be used to so I want to discuss that here before we dive in.

The numbers that you see on the diagram below are called "scale degrees", which are the names that we are going to call each note in the scale. I want to give you a way of understanding what these scales are that will allow you to use them much more intuitively than if they were just a bunch of dots on a fretboard. And if you just want to learn the scale patterns and not worry about what the numbers mean that is OK too, but this is how I like to teach and it seems to be pretty effective with my students when we work on fretboard theory.

Using the numbers instead of dots on the fretboard for where you put your fingers will hopefully show you how to start seeing where ideas can be and *are* repeated in the scale. Remember that there are only 5 notes in a pentatonic scale and one added to that for a blues scale (the b5). The amount of repetition that happens is huge in an average solo and if you start seeing the scales this way you'll also start being able to move your own licks around.

First of all, the numbers. They are what we discussed in the very beginning of this book when we talked about chord progressions. A minor or Blues scale will have different relative distances between notes to make their sounds though so we need to alter this a bit.

Major Scale Notes	C	D	E	F	G	A	B
Major Scale Degrees	1	2	3	4	5	6	7
Minor Scale Notes	C	D	Eb	F	G	Ab	Bb
Minor Scale Degrees	1	2	minor 3	4	5	minor 6	minor 7
Minor Pentatonic Notes	C		Eb	F	G		Bb
Minor Pentatonic Degrees	C		minor 3	4	5		minor 7

If a scale degree is "minor" it means that you are lowering the note one half step or one fret on the guitar. For our scale patterns below a minor 3rd is written as "m3". If you notice above the Minor pentatonic scale is the same as the Minor scale except that we have removed the 2nd and 6th notes. For a "Blues Scale" we add the "diminished 5" between the 4 and the 5. I'm also replacing the "1" with an "R" for "Root" since that is also the root of the scale and any chords that we'll be building from this.

C Blues Scale

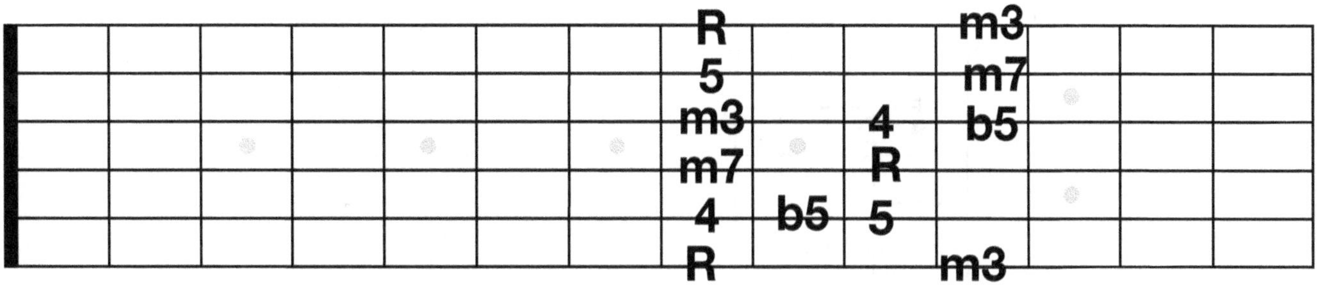

If you want to use this scale in another key then move the whole pattern down until the root of the pattern is on the root of the key you want. The blues scale on the previous page is in the key of C since the root is on the C on the 8th fret 6th string. The scales on the next page have been moved into other positions to fit them into the guitar necks. They are NOT all in the same key.

The CAGED System

This is a system of organizing your fretboard into smaller sections based off of your open chords. The first thing that we will do is to take the root of each chord out of the shapes for your open C, open A, open G, open E and open D shapes (the so-called "campfire chords" that most of us learn when first pick up a guitar). It is a great place to start but you definitely want to start connecting these patterns into one larger neck pattern sooner rather than later so that you have a more complete ability to play anywhere in any key on the guitar.

The open dots are the roots for each chord. You'll notice that for the A, G, E and D chords there are roots that fall on open strings and the "o" for a root is larger than the "0" for the normal open string fingering indication. On the next page we have the root patterns written out horizontally on guitar necks for you to see how they all lay out to play a C# note all over the fretboard. If you play the patterns in order they spell out the word "CAGED" with their chord names. You'll also see that every note is part of two root shapes...one above it and one below it on the fretboard.

Once you are comfortable with these shapes we can move on to learning each of the scales that I use on a fairly regular basis to play this music. Not every sound is in this book but these will get you through most blues, rock and soul playing situations.

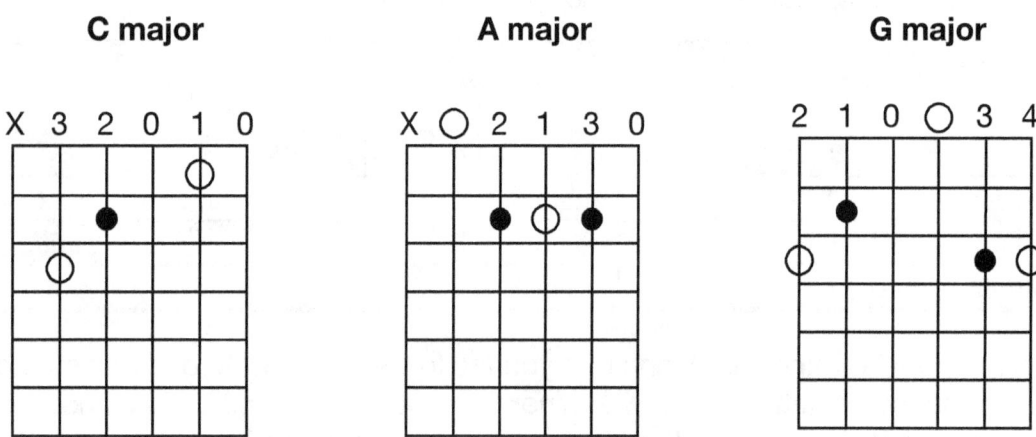

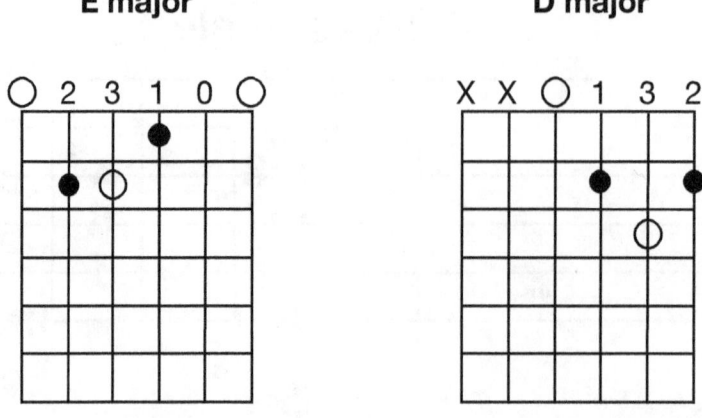

Blues Scale

E Shape

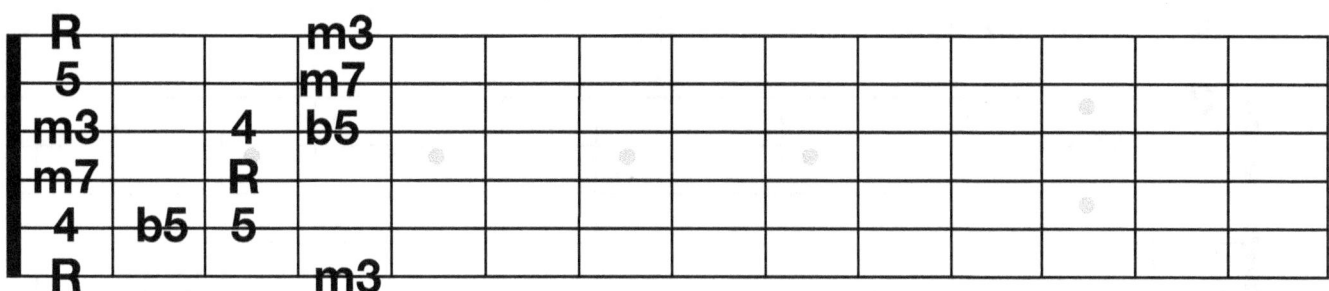

D Shape

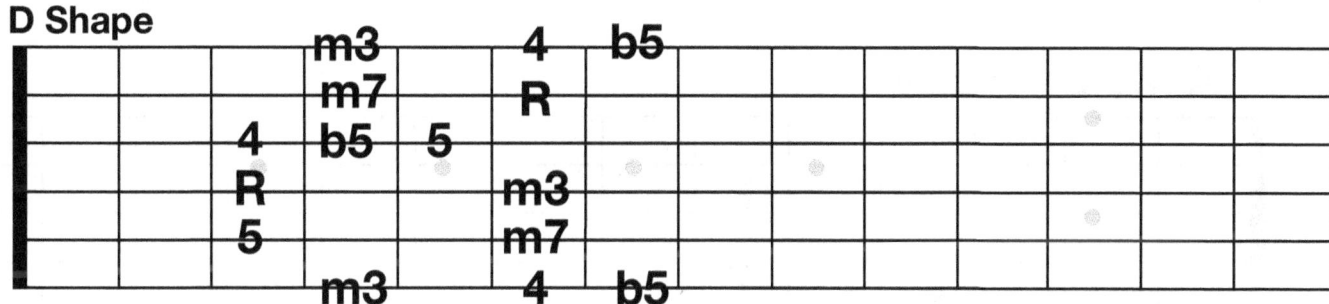

C Shape

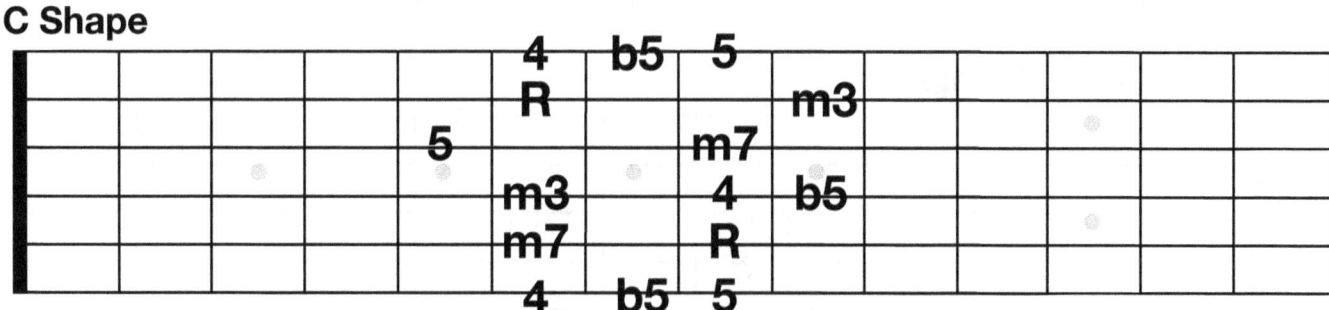

A Shape

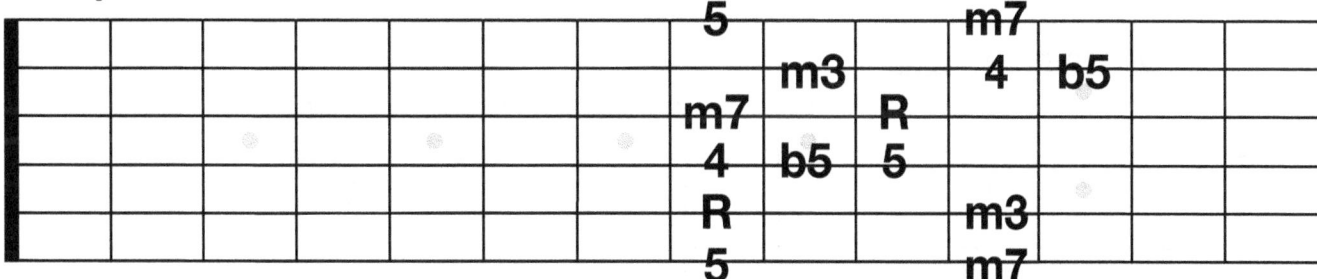

G Shape

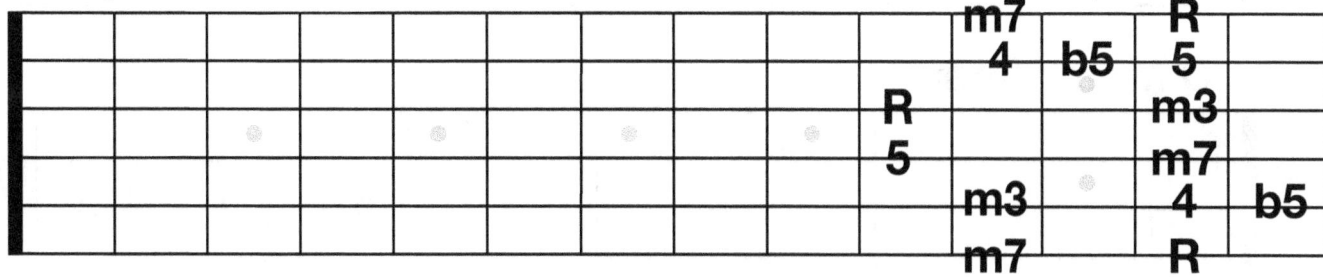

Major Triads

C Major Shape

A Major Shape

G Major Shape

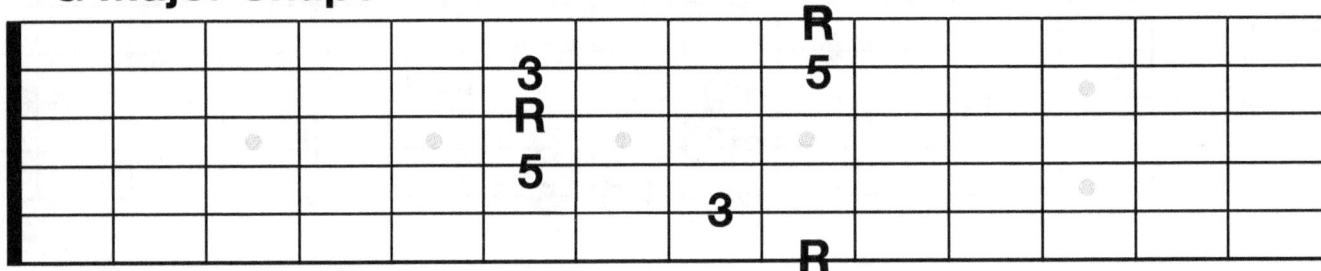

E Major Shape

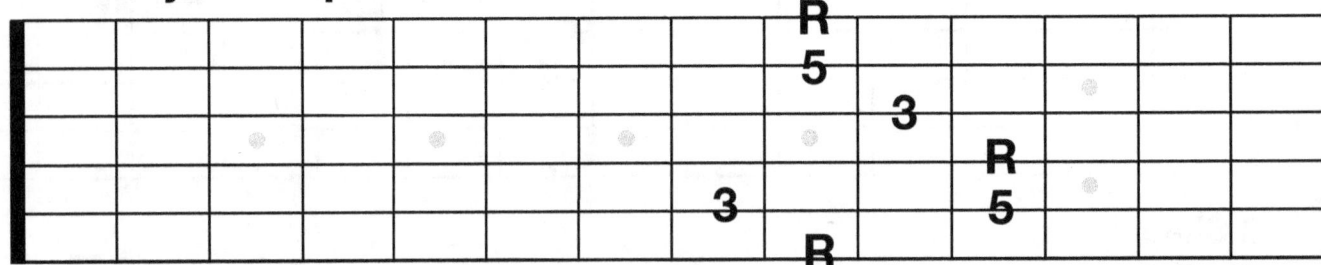

D Major Shape

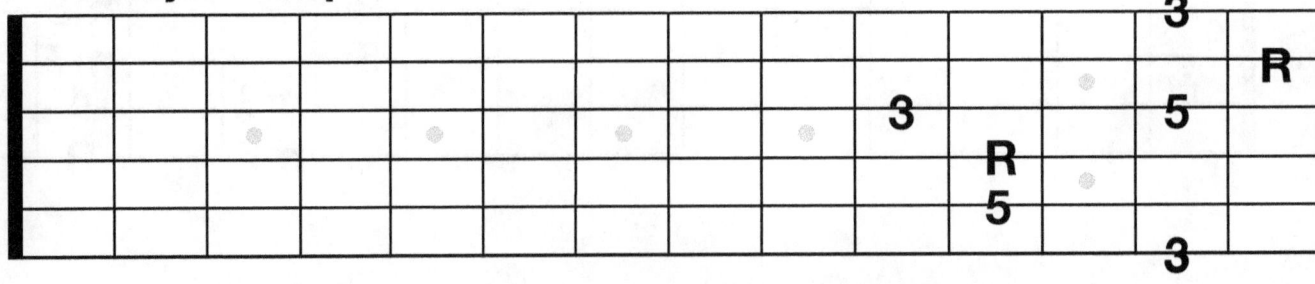

Major Scale

C Shape

```
3   4       5
7   R       2
5       6
2       3   4
6       7   R
3   4       5
```

A Shape

```
        5   6
        2   3   4
    6       R
    3   4   5
    7   R   2
        5   6
```

G Shape

```
            6       7   R
            3   4       5
        7   R       2
            5       6
            2       3   4
            6       7   R
```

E Shape

```
                7   R       2
                    5       6
                2       3   4
                6       7   R
                3   4       5
                7   R       2
```

D Shape

```
                            2       3   4
                            6       7   R
                        3   4       5
                        7   R       2
                            5       6
                            2       3   4
```

43

Major Pentatonic

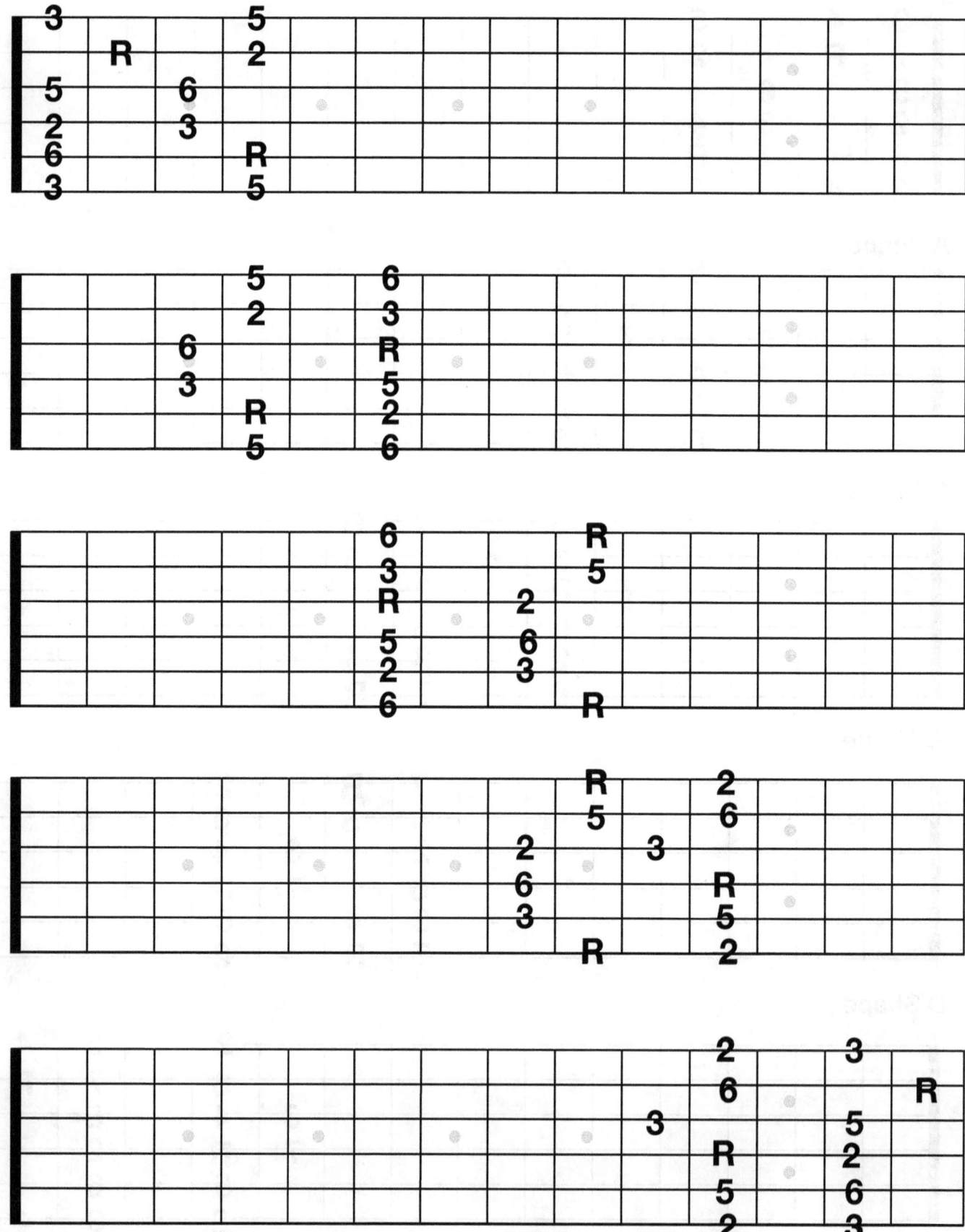

Mixolydian Scale
For Dominant Chords

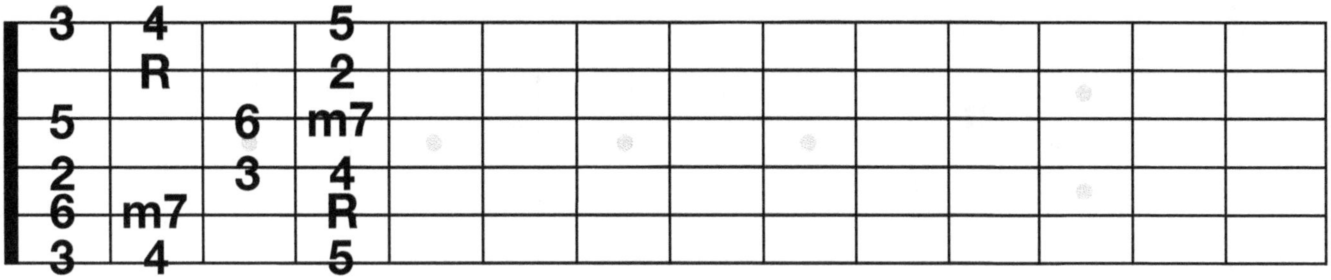

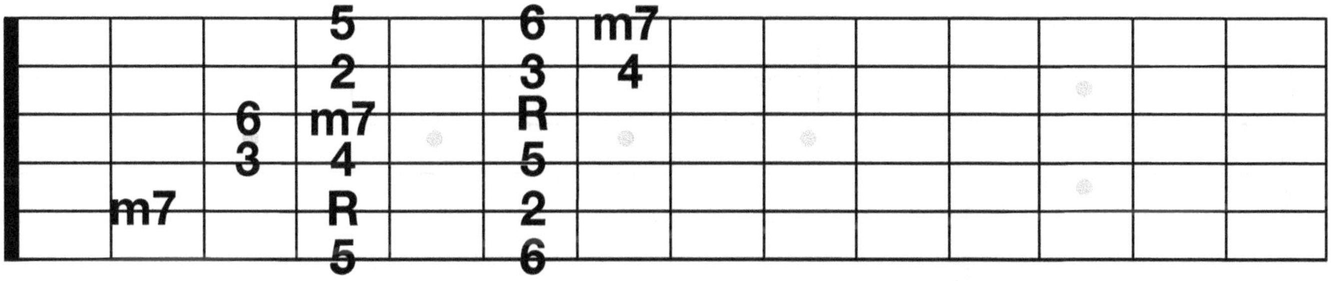

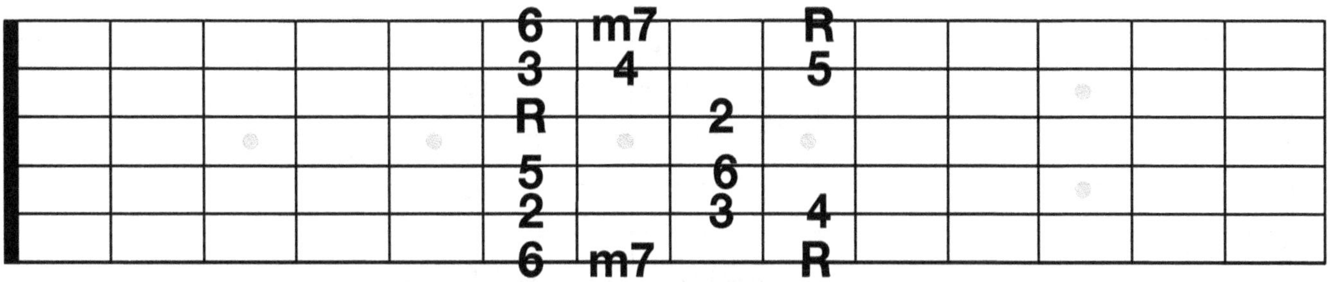

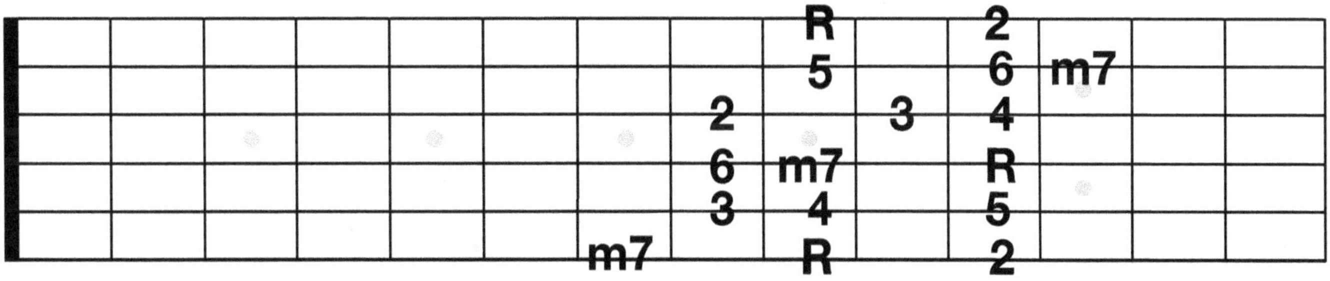

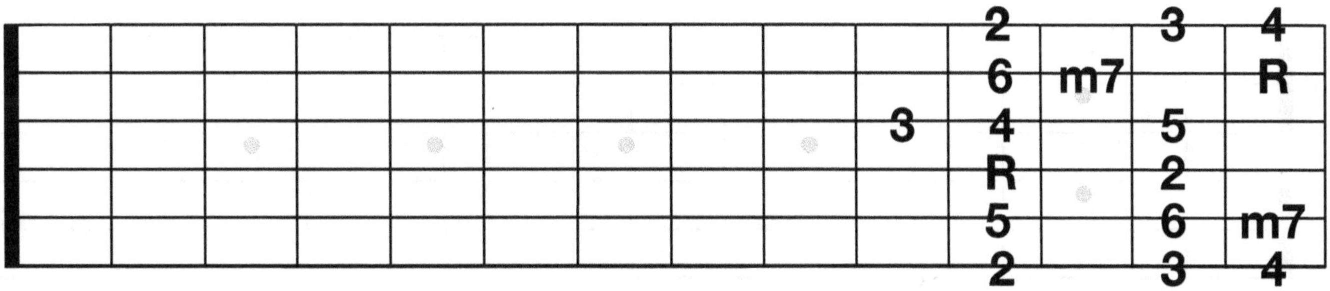

Dominant 7th Chord Tones

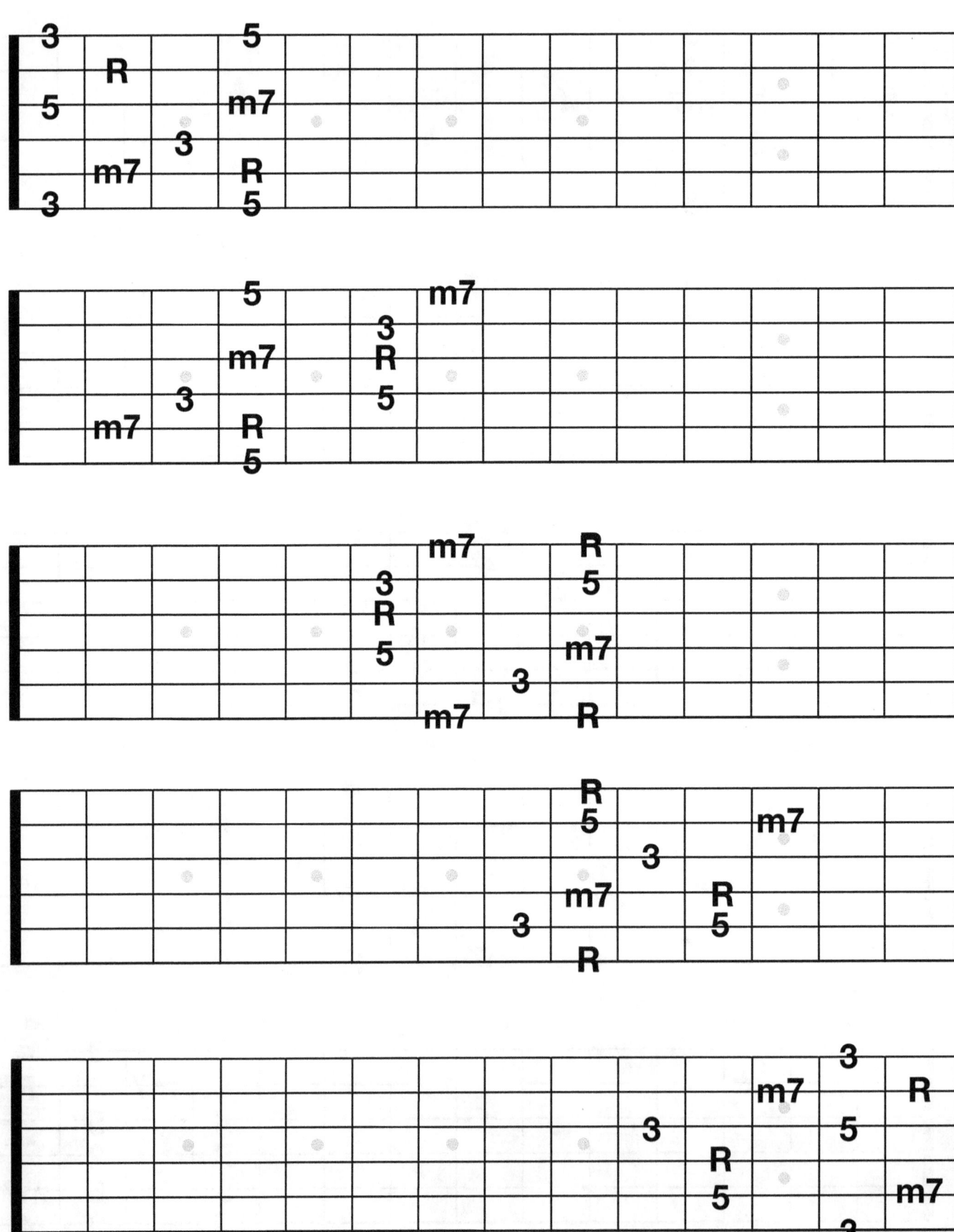

The "3 phrase" approach to soloing.

One way that I like to structure single chorus solos (or the first chorus of a longer solo) is to feel the chord progression the same way that we broke a 12 bar blues down in three 4 measure phrases earlier in the book. If you listen to a BB King or Albert King solo from one of their classic albums you can hear this approach used by the greats. Since we are working on songs from my album I figured that the intro solo from "I'm Gonna Leave" would be a good example.

I tend to play somewhat busier lines in this solo but you can still hear the structure that we are talking about. If you can listen along to the recording of this song while reading the music you will hear the "question and answer" structure pretty easily:

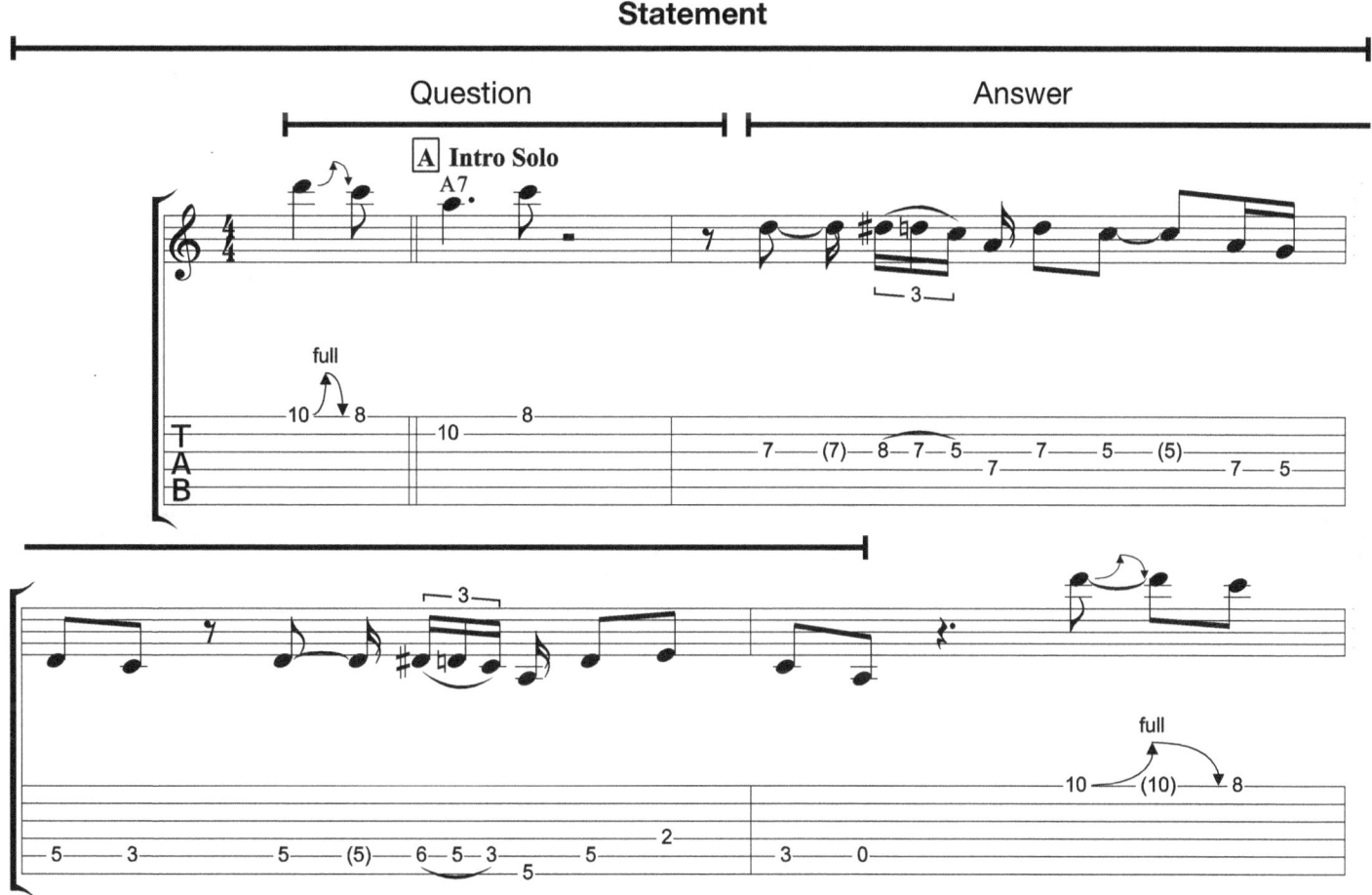

Re-Statement

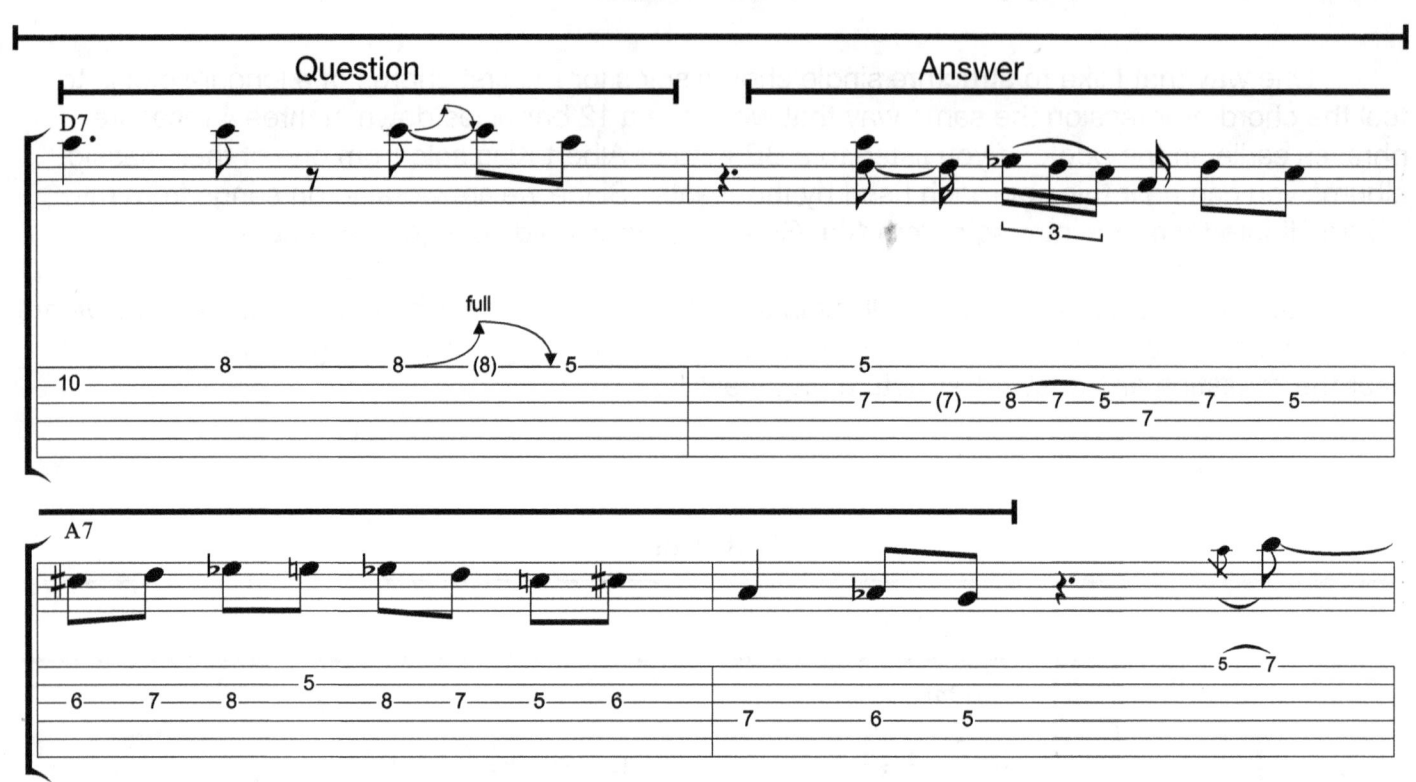

Punchline

Chromatics and Chords Tones for Dominant Chords

One idea that I really like to use to get away from playing pentatonic scales over everything is to take the chord tones from a dominant 7th chord and build lines around them. If you just play the chord tones its a pretty boring sound though so I like to spice them up with chromatic passing tones and bits of the Mixolydian scale.

The easiest way to apply this concept is to connect two chord tones (such as the m7th and the root or the 3rd and the 5th) with all of the notes in between. I've got some examples to illustrate this idea over an A7 chord. I've circled the chord tones in the examples to make it easier for you to see how the idea lays out.

This first example is from the intro solo to "I'm Gonna Leave". The second line is a variation.

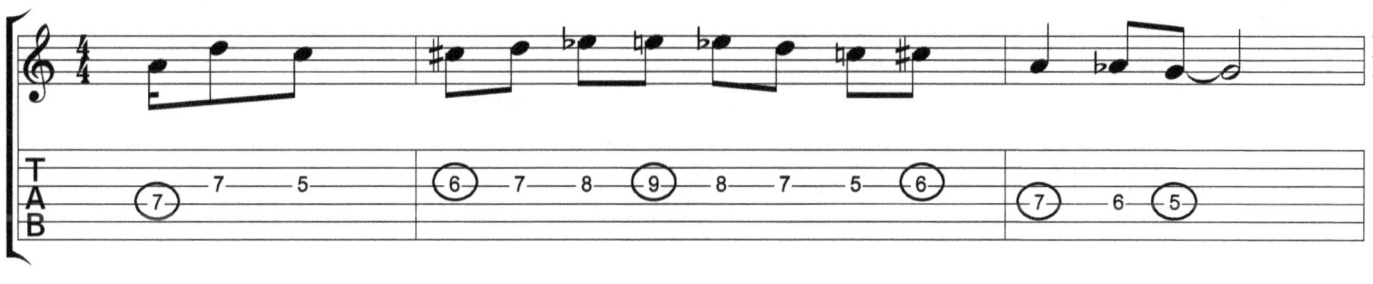

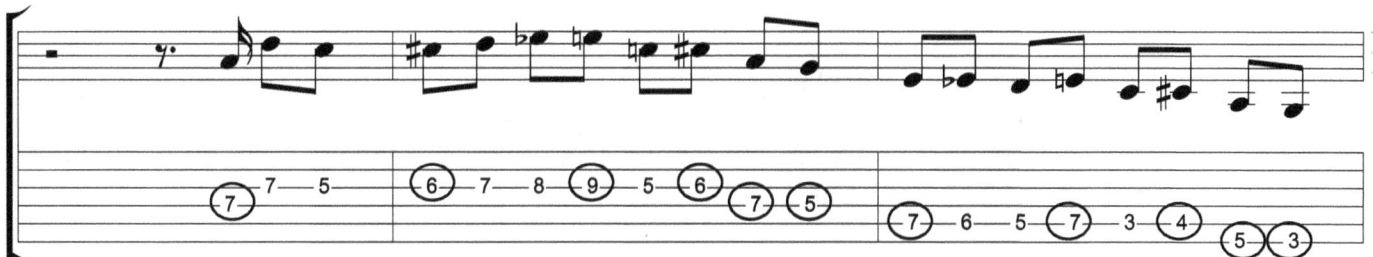

Example 2 - Play a scale tone above each note and a half step below. I think I stole this idea from a Les Paul recording when I was in college.

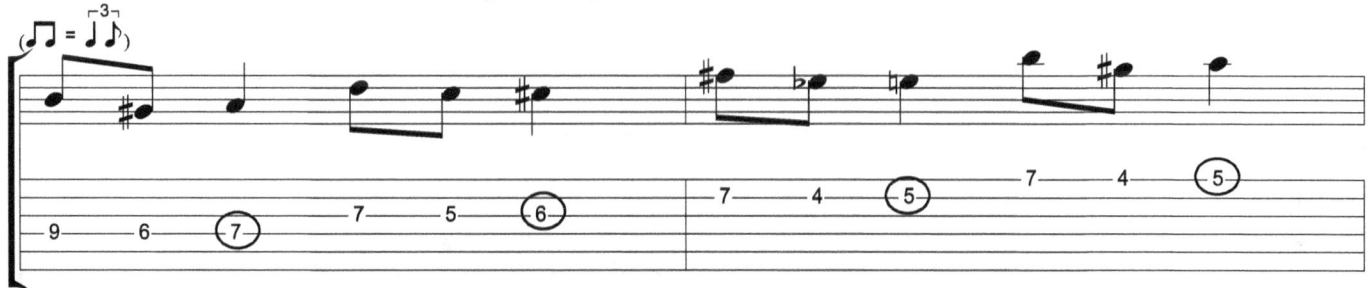

Example 3 - The articulation in the first half of each measure is similar to example 2.

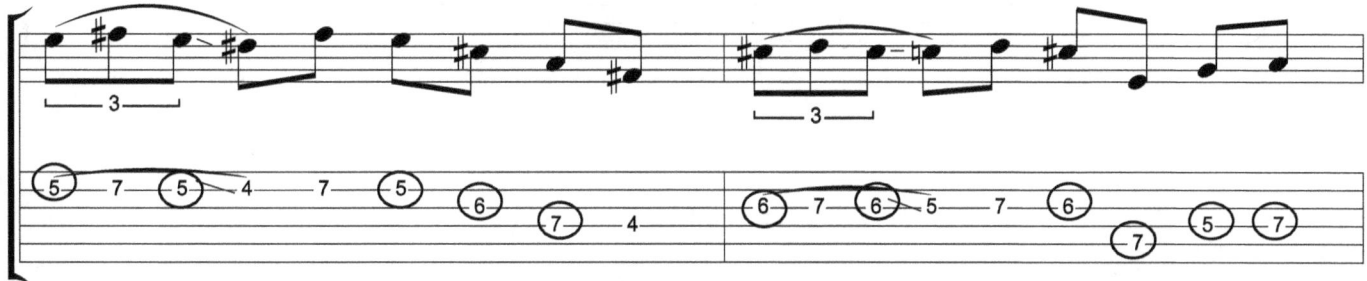

Example 4

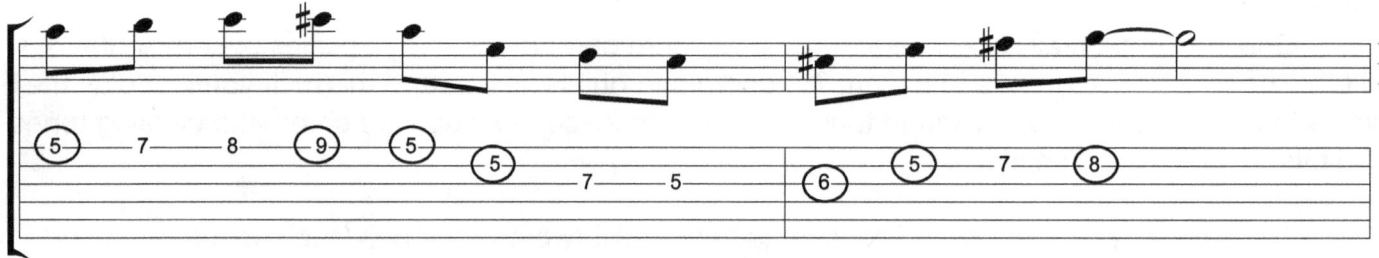

Example 5 - this lick is similar to the verse fills from "Roar". I'm just sliding the notes of the chord two at a time down a half step and then back up to fit the chord.

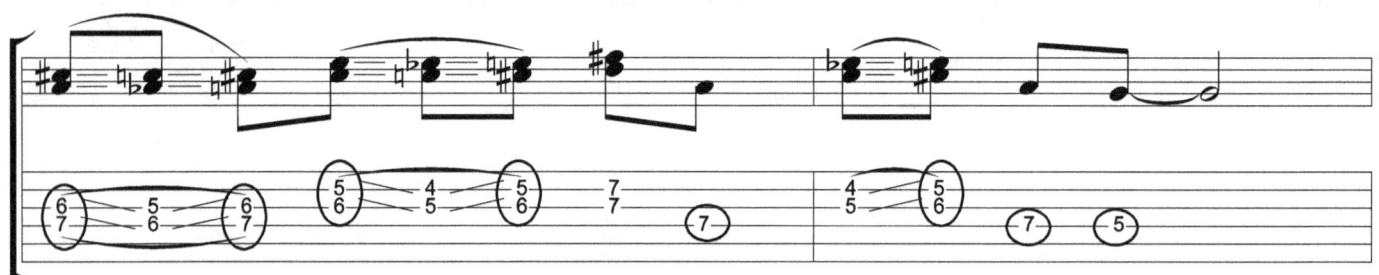

Examples 6 and 7 - I don't play anything like this on the album but they are full of ideas that I also like to play over an A7 chord so I figured I would share them here. Besides the ideas discussed above I also play an Em7 chord over the A7 and resolve to a C# in both ideas. Look for the E, G, B and D notes in the second beat of #6 and the first beat of #7.

Example 6

Example 7

Section 3

• • •

Song Examples

Extended Pentatonic Scale Patterns

Most of the soloing for our first song is in the A Blues scale. I'm going to give you the standard scale pattern first.

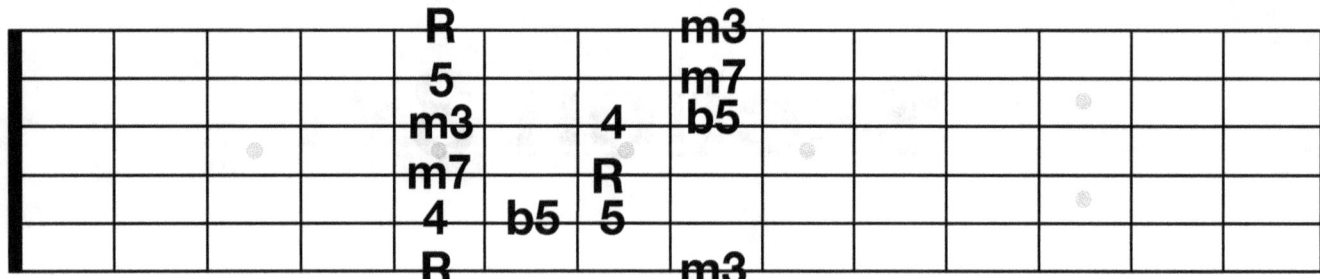

This pattern however more accurately shows how I play the scale. The more diagonal approach helps me play lines that feel more musical to me. If you look you can also see that each set of two strings gives you the same pattern from the m7 to the 5 on the next string. I like to play an idea in one of those "sub patterns" and then answer it in a pattern above or below it to make a line sound more vocal. In the example below I have the first and third permutations of the pattern bracketed for you to more easily see what I am talking about.

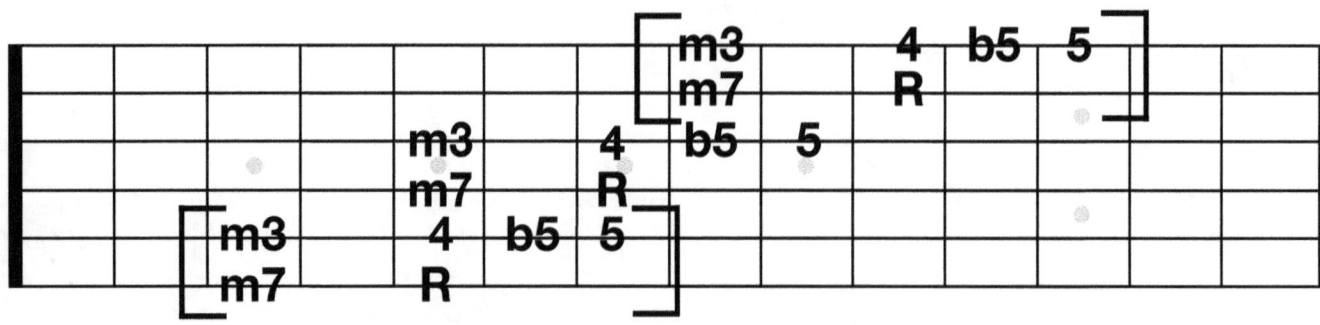

I try to play most of my lines in extended or diagonal directions on the fretboard. Most scales can be worked to play this way pretty easily. We will have a major pentatonic version of this in the next song. You can also arrange your major, minor or other diatonic scales like this if you play them three notes to the string.

I'm Gonna Leave

"I'm Gonna Leave" is a 12 Bar Blues in the key of A. The feel is kind of a modified Boogaloo. For this record we tried to do some of my favorite feels but to give them something other than a stock rendering of the gooves and chord progressions. I play all of the solos in this song but the rhythm guitar is played by my friend Tommy Harkenrider and he plays some great melodic but still in-the-pocket ideas. The intro solo is very influenced by Albert King but I end up a little more in Albert Lee territory by the middle of the main solo. Maybe if you slowed an Albert Lee recording down to half speed and gave him some strong cough syrup or something like that.

A few notes about the rest of the solo.

1. The second chorus starts with me playing a 3 note A7 chord shape that moves around into other two and three note bits. Those are all "hybrid picked", which is where you hold the pick between your thumb and index finger for the third string and use your middle and ring fingers for the second and first string respectively.

2. The tremolo picking in the 9th bar of the second chorus of solo (its over the E7 chord) is difficult to get at first because you are picking as quick as you can on the second string but you need to slide into the 5th fret on each beat to get it in time.

3. The pull-off lick in the last couple of bars is most definitely not a bluesy lick but it seemed like a fun way to wrap it up. It is played in groups of three 16th note triplets per string and there are two triplets per beat. The hard part is that it starts on the "and" of the first beat but try to keep the phrase in time and don't rush through it.

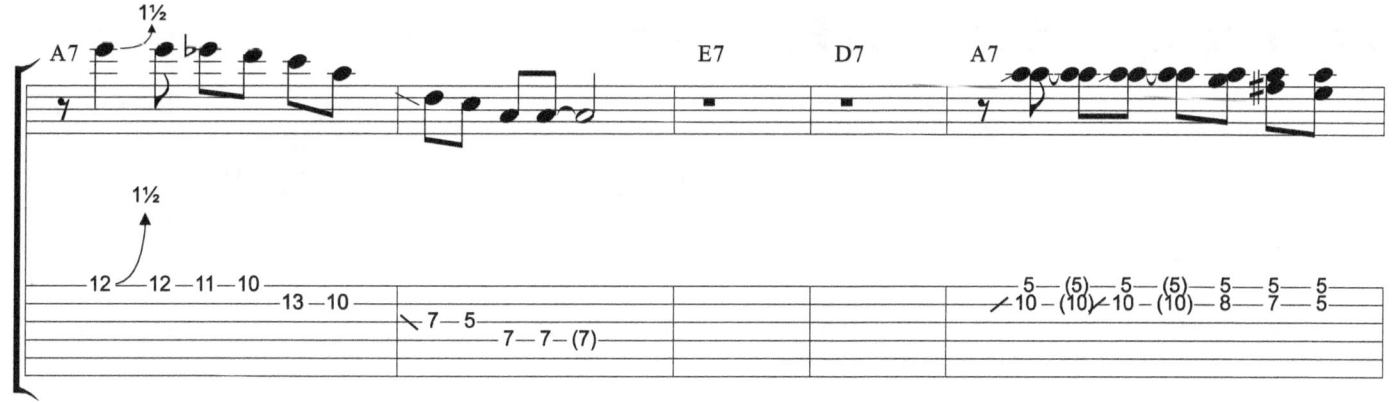

Primer page for Someone Elses' Fool

This song is an 8 bar blues. Because each chord lasts so long I tend to play more Major Pentatonic and Major chord tone ideas over it for the solos, which gives the song a somewhat more Country music feel.

The construction of a Major Pentatonic scale is similar to how we found our Minor Pentatonic. In this case we remove the 4th and 7th notes of a major scale:

Major Scale Notes	C	D	E	F	G	A	B
Major Scale Degrees	1	2	3	4	5	6	7
Major Pentatonic Scale Notes	C	D	E		G	A	
Major Pentatonic Scale Degrees	1	2	3		5	6	
Major Chord Notes	C		E		G		
Major Chord Degrees	C		3		5		

You will also notice that the Major Chord notes and Scale degrees are added to the chart above. One concept that is incredibly important to me is that when playing a scale you should know what the parent triad or chord tones are. A major chord can be found by taking the Root, 3rd and 5th notes of a major scale. You can do the same thing with a minor scale too. Those notes are the easiest way to define the sound of a scale so that you're just not playing up and down a bunch of notes with no real melody or phrasing. I try to use those notes as a "skeleton" or inner framework of a scale sound. In rock, pop and blues settings I try to resolve my phrases to a chord tone as much as possible. The non-chord tone notes in the scale are great for creating tension in your idea...if you want to make an interesting phrase think of it as a "question and answer" type of conversation. When a person asks a question the pitch of their voice gives a cue as to what the sentence they just said is about. A questioning phrase usually feels unresolved and needs an answer.

Read this out loud:

"Did you take the trash out?"

"Yes, I did"

To me that is a complete melodic idea. When I solo I try to have bits that create tension and then resolve even within longer phrases. Play a lick in a scale and end on the 2nd, 4th, 6th or 7th note of a major scale. Then play the same idea but end on the root, 3rd or 5th. What do your ears tell you?

This is not the only way to solo and its more of a lesson in phrasing than in describing what I do in this song but I really want you to think about this stuff if you start learning my solo phrases. You will find that what makes them work is that they are specific to the chord they are being played over, and this is a hallmark of soloing or improvising in Country, Jazz, Bluesgrass and to a lesser extent Blue music. To me it is important to know scales but it is far more important to know the notes of the chords you are playing over. And then how to embellish them appropriately for the style.

So here is a Major Pentatonic scale in its most popular pattern. It looks exactly like the first Minor Pentatonic scale we learned in the last song, but the numbers are all different. Be careful that you don't just play your A minor pentatonic licks down three frets and think that you are playing in A major. Your minor scale ideas probably resolve to the chord tone of a minor chord in that pattern, which are NOT the same as the chord tones for the major sound. Use your ears when you play!!!

In the outro solo I play this extended version of that scale. In the last song where I had a Minor Pentatonic scale that allowed me to play more on the diagonal we now have the same concept for the Major Pentatonic. Here is that scale as it lays out in two places on the fretboard in A:

61

Another idea that I really like to use in a Major Pentatonic scale for this kind of playing is to add the 4th back into the scale from the Major scale. I usually don't sit on it very long but it tends to help me be a bit more vocal in my phrasing. Look for this idea in the very first measure of the solo.

```
|---3---4-------5-----------------------3---4-------5---------|
|---R-----------------------------------R-----------2---------|
|-------------2-------------------------------------6---------|
|-------------6-----------------------------------------------|
|-------------------------------------------------------------|
|-------------------------------------------------------------|
```

Oblique Bends and Hybrid Picking

Again with this song we have a few things that are a little different. An "Oblique Bend" is a bend where we fret two notes on adjoining strings and bend one to another pitch while keeping the other one unbent and in tune. Not always the easiest thing to do until you get the hang of it. In this example you are fretting the 5th fret 2nd string with your little finger (4th) while bending the 4th fret 3rd string with your ring finger (3rd). After you release the bend you'll pull off to the 2nd fret on the 3rd string (which is played with the 1st finger).

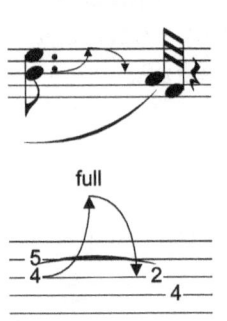

Before Bending

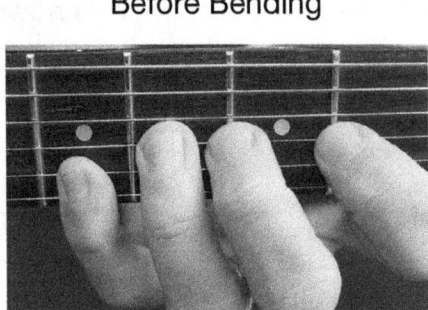

While Bending

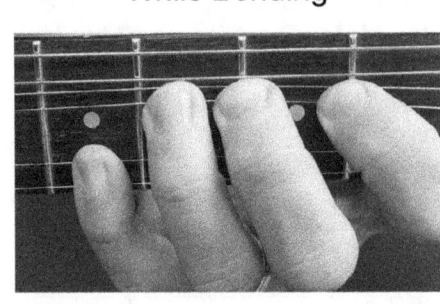

I also hybrid pick the 6ths in ideas like this one. In this context "6th" refers to the distance between two notes. That is what we call an "interval". The number refers to how many scale tones are involved. A sixth up from C is A: C, D, E ,F, G, A. A sixth up from D is B: D, E ,F, G, A, B. Just count all of the notes involved. Once again, not a complete lesson in harmony but I think it gets the idea across well enough for our needs.

Starting at the third 16th note in the example below you see notes played at the same time on the 2nd and 4th strings that are a 6th apart in pitch. I pick everything on the 4th string with my pick and everything on the 2nd string with my middle finger. The one note on the 1st string is played with the ring finger on the picking hand.

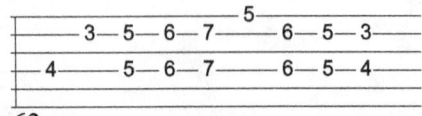

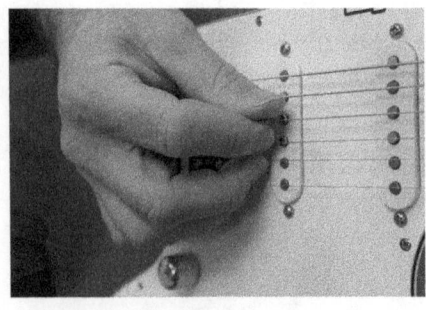

Someone Else's Fool

This is an 8 bar blues in the key of A. I play the bottom part while singing and Tommy Harkenrider plays the top part until I solo at which times he switches to the bottom.

One of my favorite "two guitar moments" in this song is the end of every verse where both guitar parts play different turnarounds that work nicely together. That wasn't worked out but happened during the recording process. We actually recorded both parts at the same time to get more of a live band feel when we did the overdubs on this song and I think the end result has a good atmosphere to it.

The only thing that changes as far as the chord progression goes is under the final outro solo where we we play a D minor chord in the 4th measure. Thats probably my favorite alterations to an 8 bar blues but it you use it for every chorus it can be a bit much.

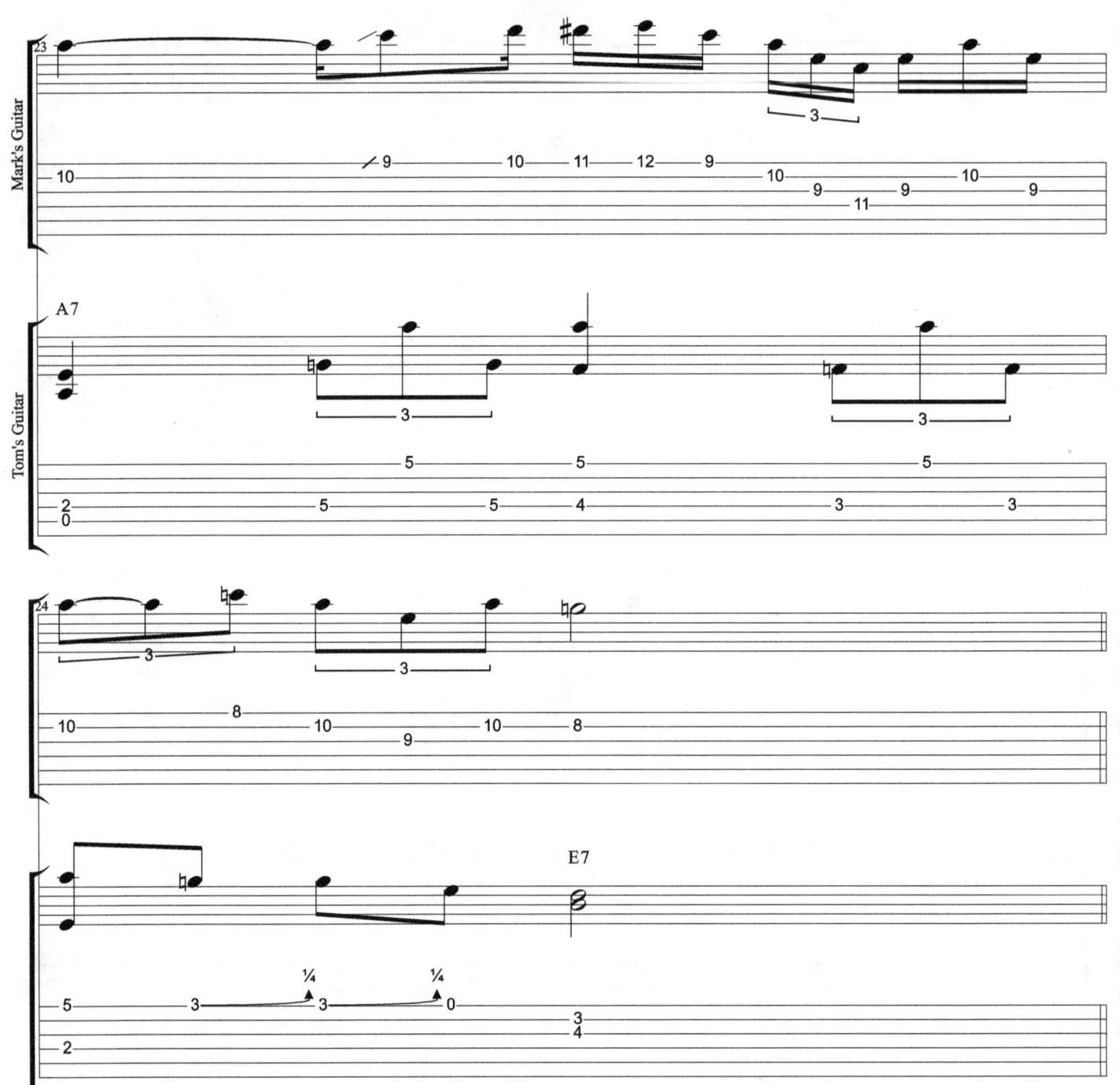

F **Outro Guitar Solo**

Roar

This song started life as something of a Jerry Lee Lewis or Chuck Berry rock and roll song. That got old pretty fast for me so I played around with some other feels and wrote the melody that makes up the instrumental "head" for the tune. The original idea was to do a Western Swing sounding guitar harmony. Think "Boston meets Bob Wills". I had to work out a way to rehearse the song with the band before we recorded it and I ended up enjoying the single guitar part more so thats how we recorded it. While recording I also ended up improvising a call and response bit between the "harmony" or double stop guitar parts.

The chord progression under the instrumental bit is not a standard 12 bar blues like the vocal verses and the solos. In the 9th bar there is a minor ii chord and the 10th bar there is a bII7 chord in place of the V and IV chords you would normally find in those bars. I liked the 1950's futuristic sound those chords gave the melody but didn't want to hear it for the entire song.

And this song has a bridge, which is not too typical for most 12 bar blues tunes, especially one where the feel is a modified Mambo/Boogaloo sort of thing.

As far as the solo goes it starts in "Chuck Berry" mode. Over the IV chord I play some of the sliding 9th chord fragments like we learned in the "complicated top" part earlier in the book and then I finish it up with some pretty standard blues licks.

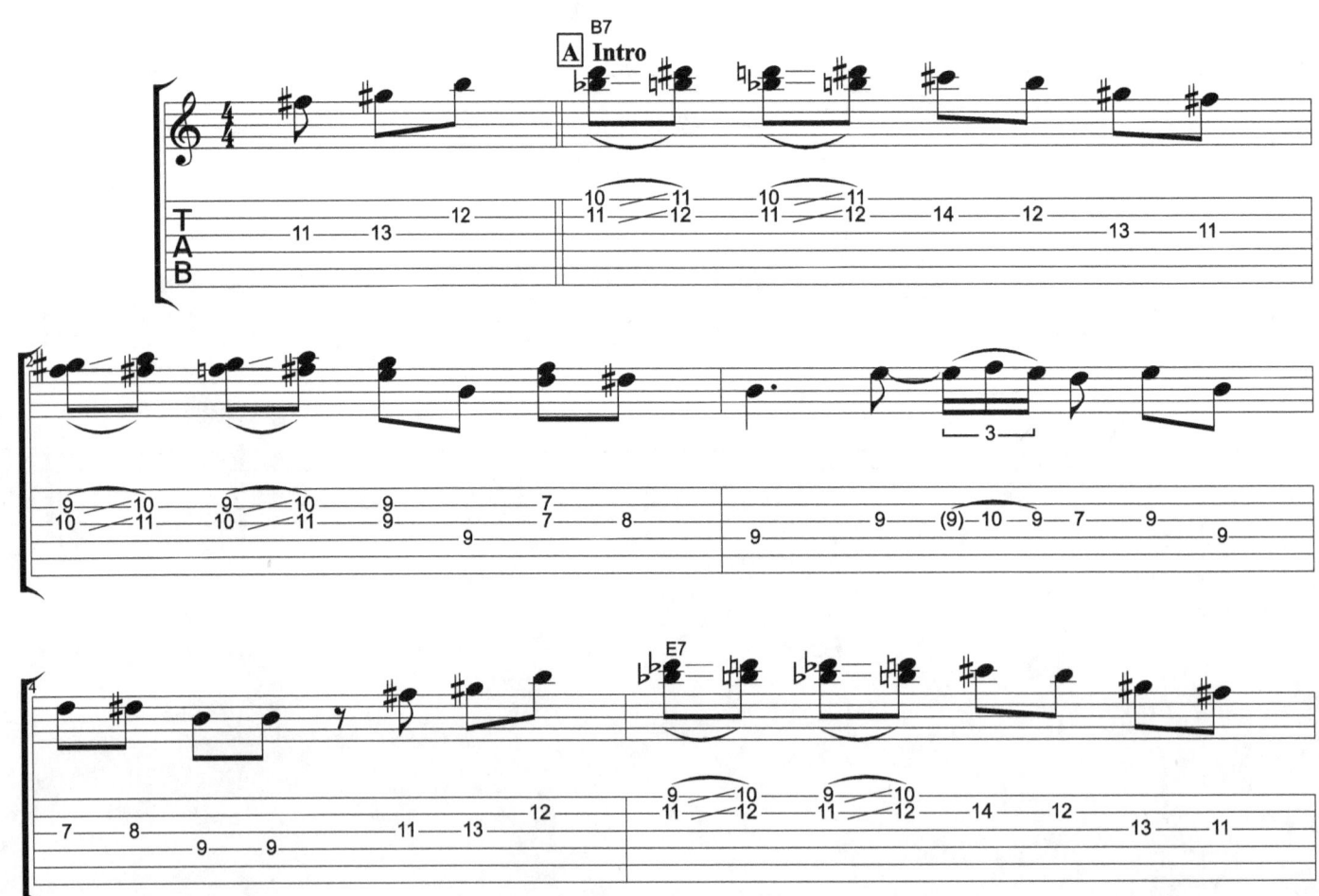

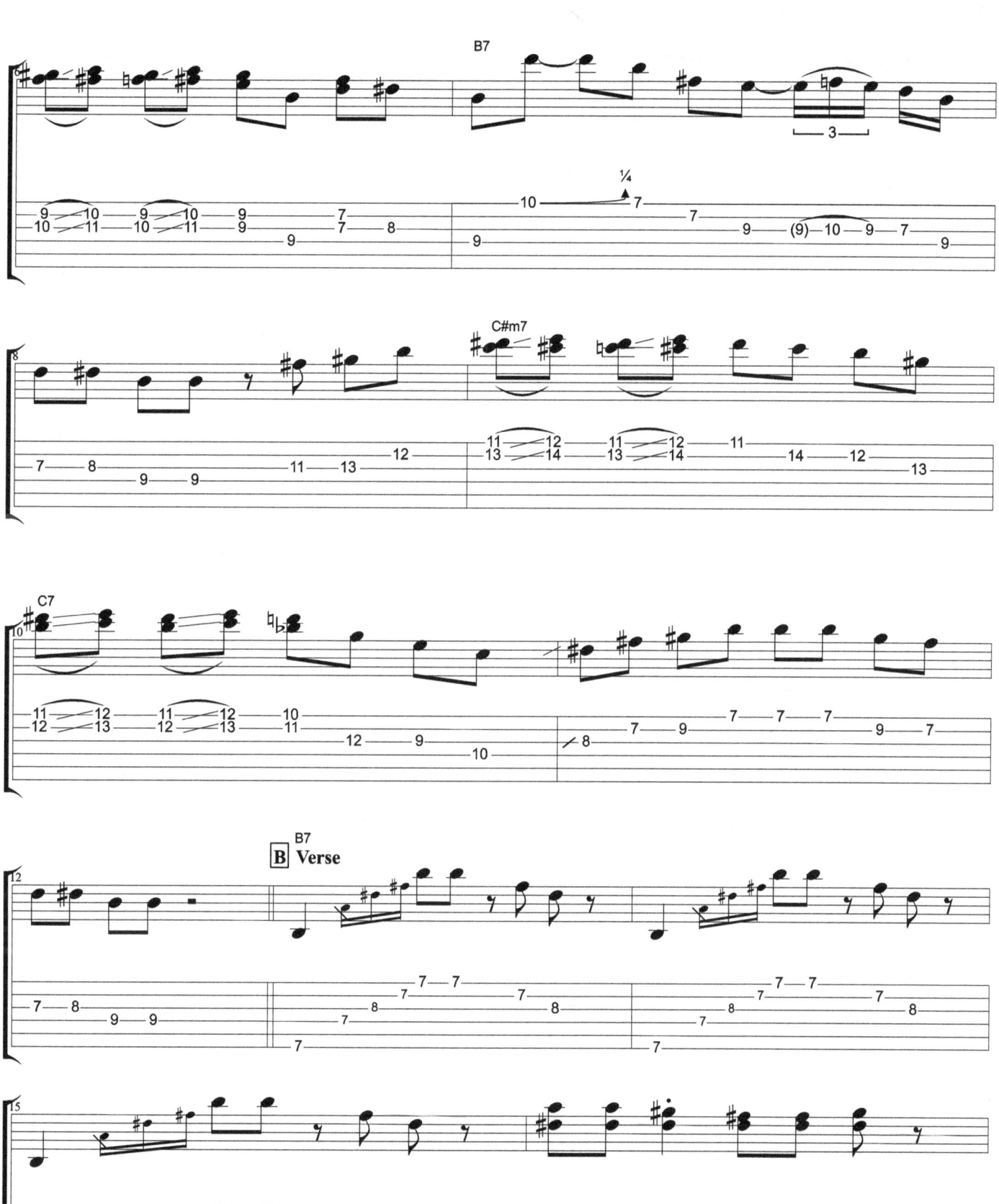

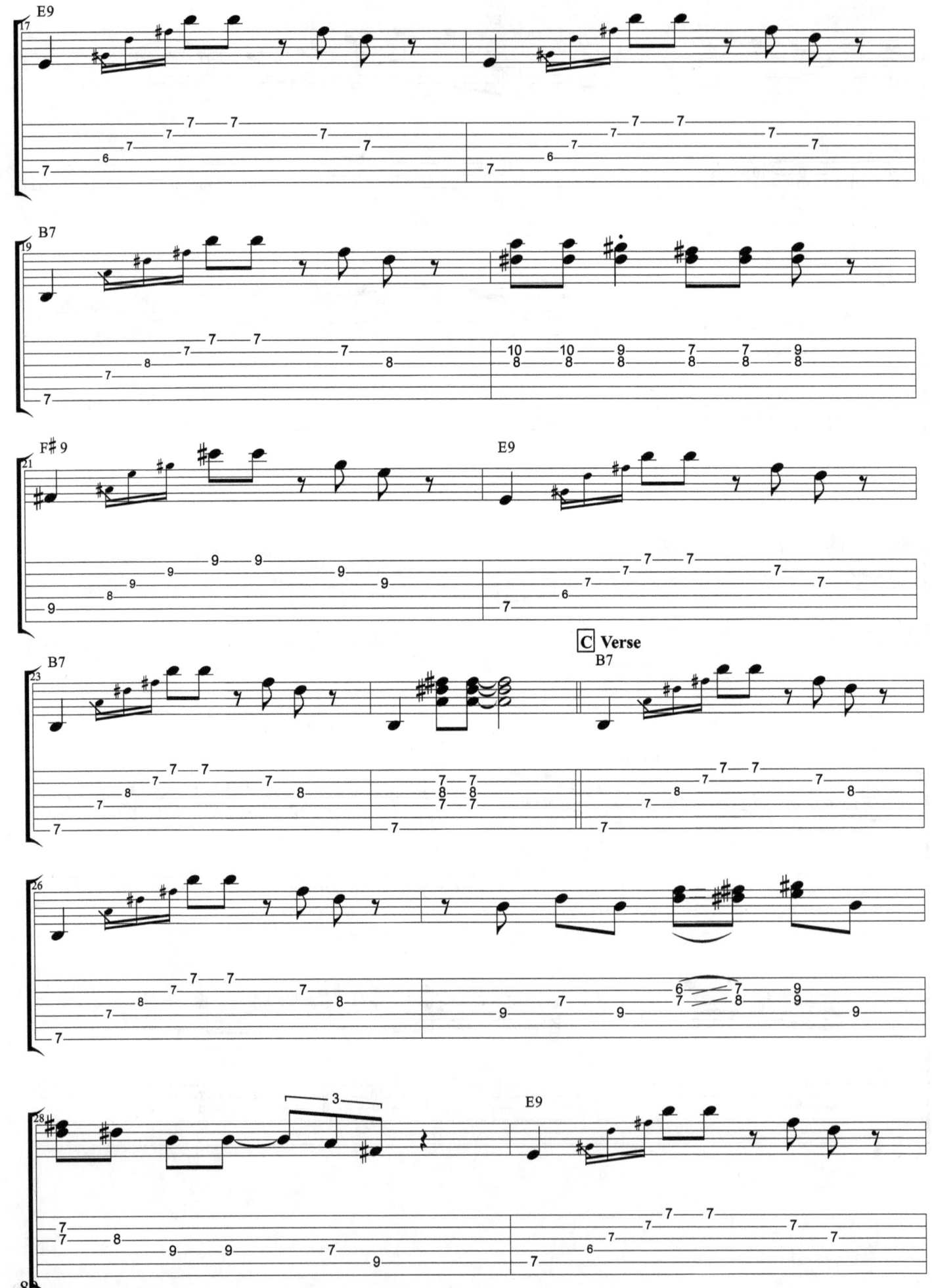

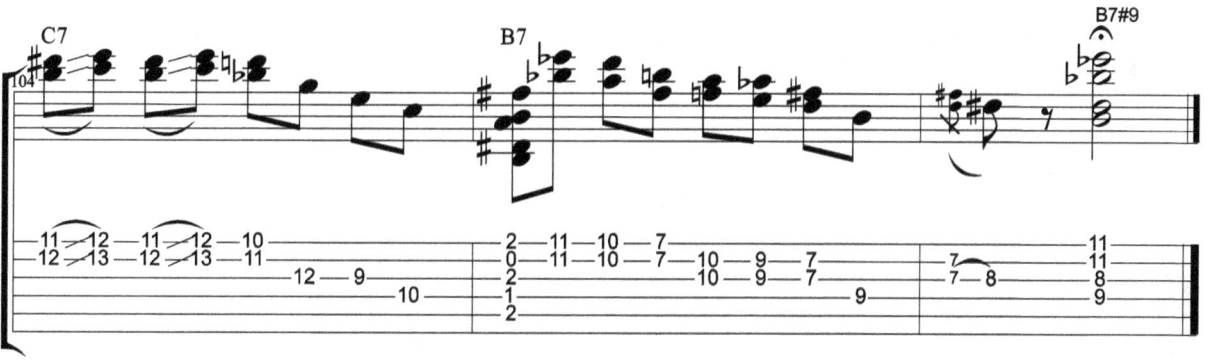

85

Can I Take You Home?

"Can I Take You Home?" has a pretty straightforward rock/soul groove. The song is in the key of Bb and the riff for the I chord is hybrid picked. I play the IV and V chords with the pick. My guitar is actually my scratch guitar part. We really didn't plan on keeping the stuff I played when we were tracking bass and drums but I liked both my rhythm part and my solo so we kept it even though I wasn't in love with the guitar tone.

There is a second "backbeat" guitar played by Scott Francisco, who actually produced the album. I really didn't want any songs with me playing both guitar parts because I wanted more of a band feel so Scott and Tommy contributed some of the extra guitars that fill these songs out. Scotts' part is transcribed after the main transcription of my parts.

The solo is a mix of major and minor pentatonic sounds. There are a lot of notes but as you try to play the longer phrases try to keep them in time...don't rush through them.

Scott's Guitar Part on "Can I Take You Home?"

  Listening to the rough mixes I realized pretty early on that I needed *something* else for the groove. I knew that a Steve Cropper sounding part would work well and that producer Scott can play that sort of part better than anyone I know so I asked him to play it on this track. Instead of the chord stabs being on every backbeat (beats 2 and 4 in a groove like this) he worked out a part where sometimes he would leave out beat 4 on the 1st bar of every 2 bar phrase on the I chord and then he's back to playing both backbeats on the IV and V chords. It integrated with my part perfectly and he used a strat with lipstick tube pickups that have the part a little more brightness that also balanced the sound of my guitar, which was from the scratch track and a little thick on its own.

  This isn't the whole song but you get 12 bars of what the two guitars look like when playing together. This song and "Everythings' Cool" both have 2nd guitar parts like this that really weave a killer groove together.

Life is Good

This song has very little guitar in it compared to the other tunes on the album. Continuing in my psuedo-latin feels for this album (I think this is closest to a Blues Mambo than anything else) I really liked the feel of the Wurlitzer keyboard with the Bass and Drums. I don't come in until the keyboard solo playing some long chords with the tremolo on my 1964 Sllvertone 1484 cranked up.

The solo actually is influnced by Jimmy Vaughan. I loved the sound of him playing with a capo and the lick he does where he slides into the 5th fret on the 2nd string while plaing the same note open on the first string is one of my favorites. I don't use a capo on this so you have to make a pretty wide stretch at the beginning of the guitar solo. Use your first finger on the 1st string 3rd fret and slide your pinky on the 2nd string into the 8th fret. I'm also hybrid picking most of the two note licks in this solo. The last verse continues with some licks in response to the vocals to the ending.

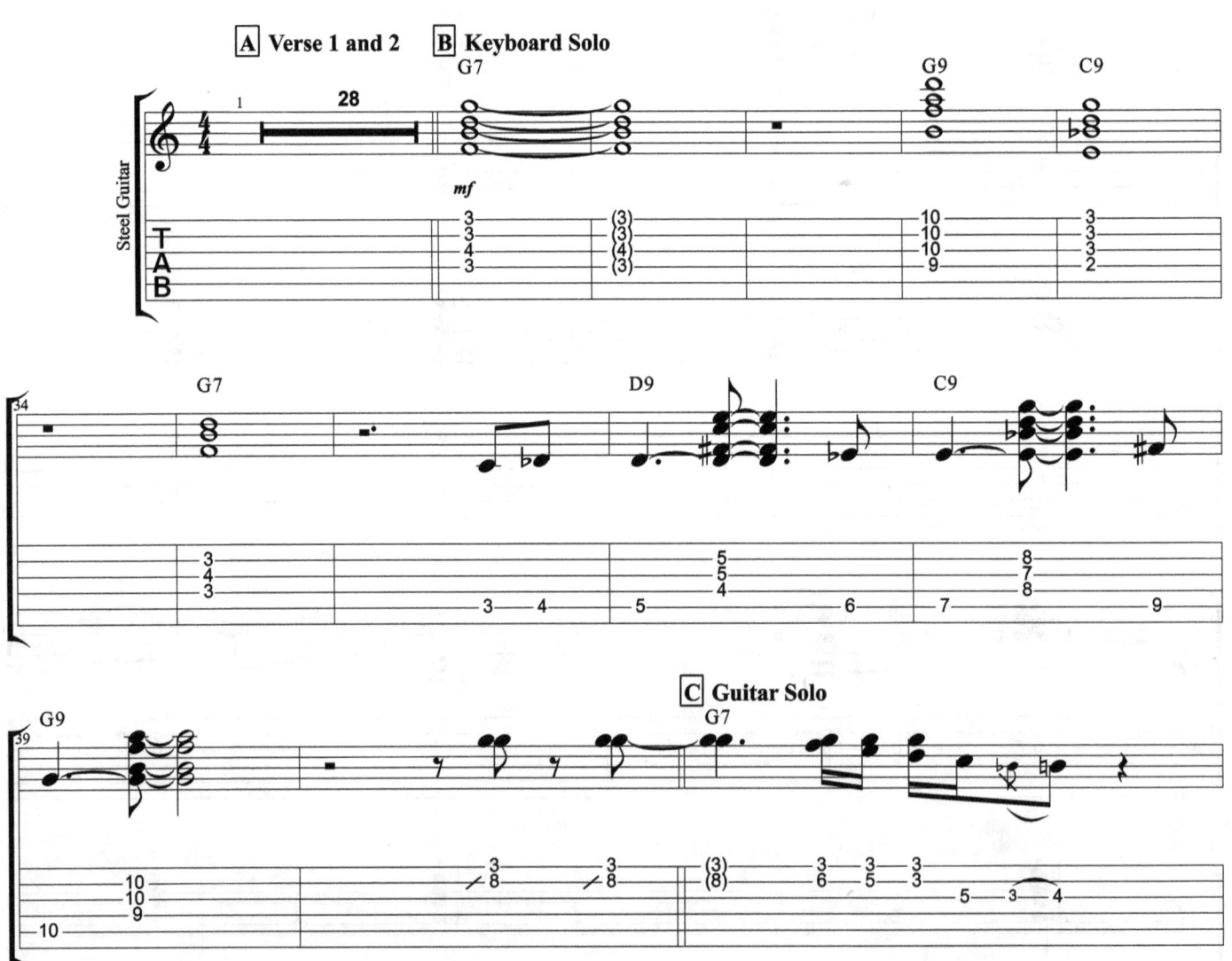

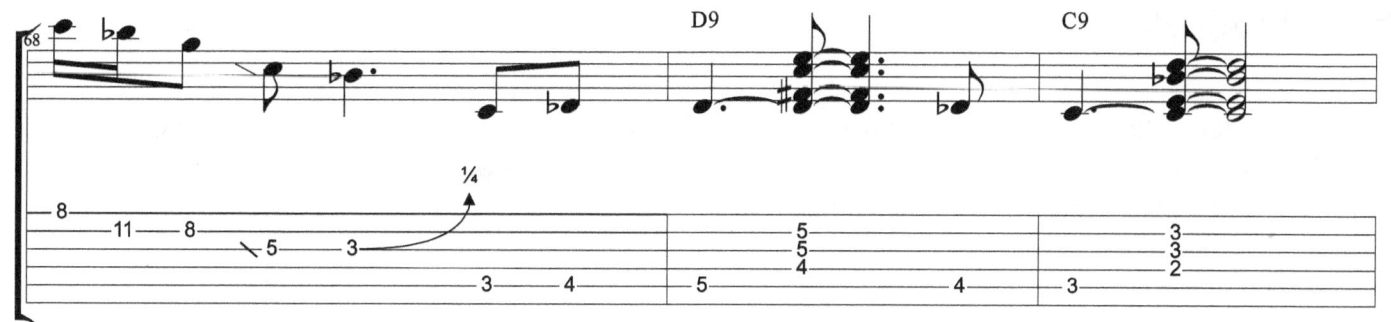
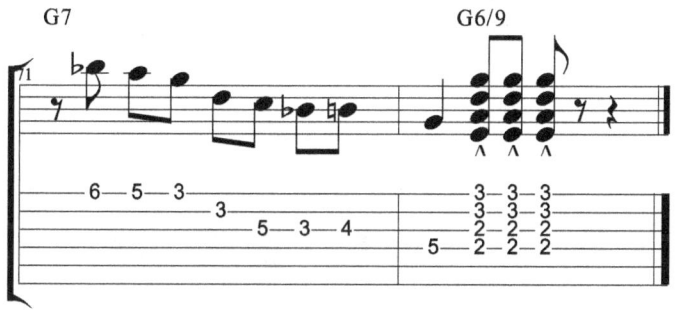

95

Black Market Hearts

Black Market Hearts is a 12 bar blues chord progression with groove born in New Orleans. I love Second Line-style drum grooves and really wanted to include one on this album so when I started playing around with the rhythm guitar part in this song it was definitely a no-brainer for me.

The one thing that might be difficult for you in this song is the rhythm guitar part, so we will take a look right now. This is a 16th note based groove that is has a swing or shuffled 16th note feel. I am putting a single measure of the groove with strum directions here for you to work on. Remember that the "X"s in the tab are muted notes. Just release the chord voicing enough to make a scratch sound when you strum.

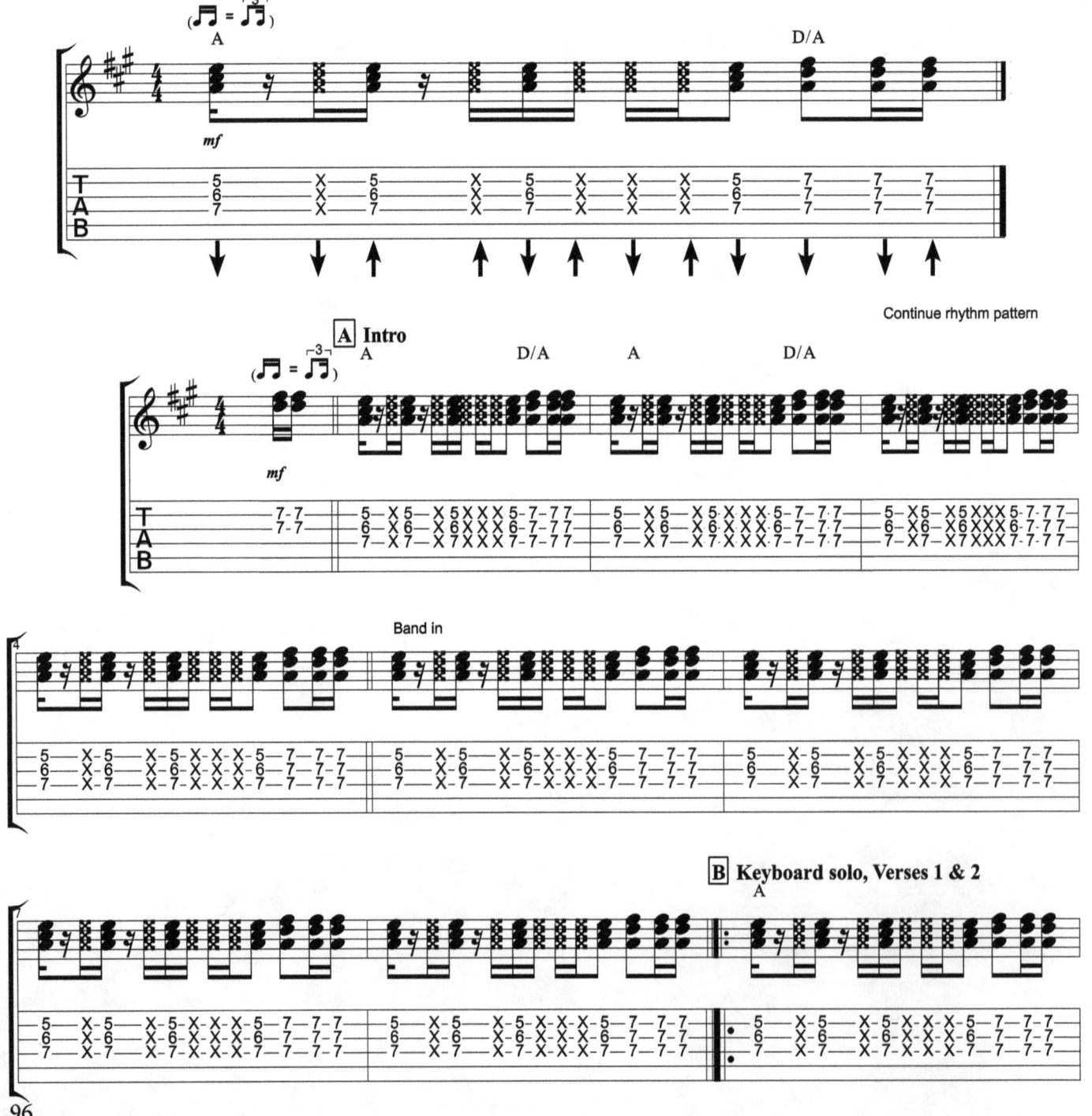

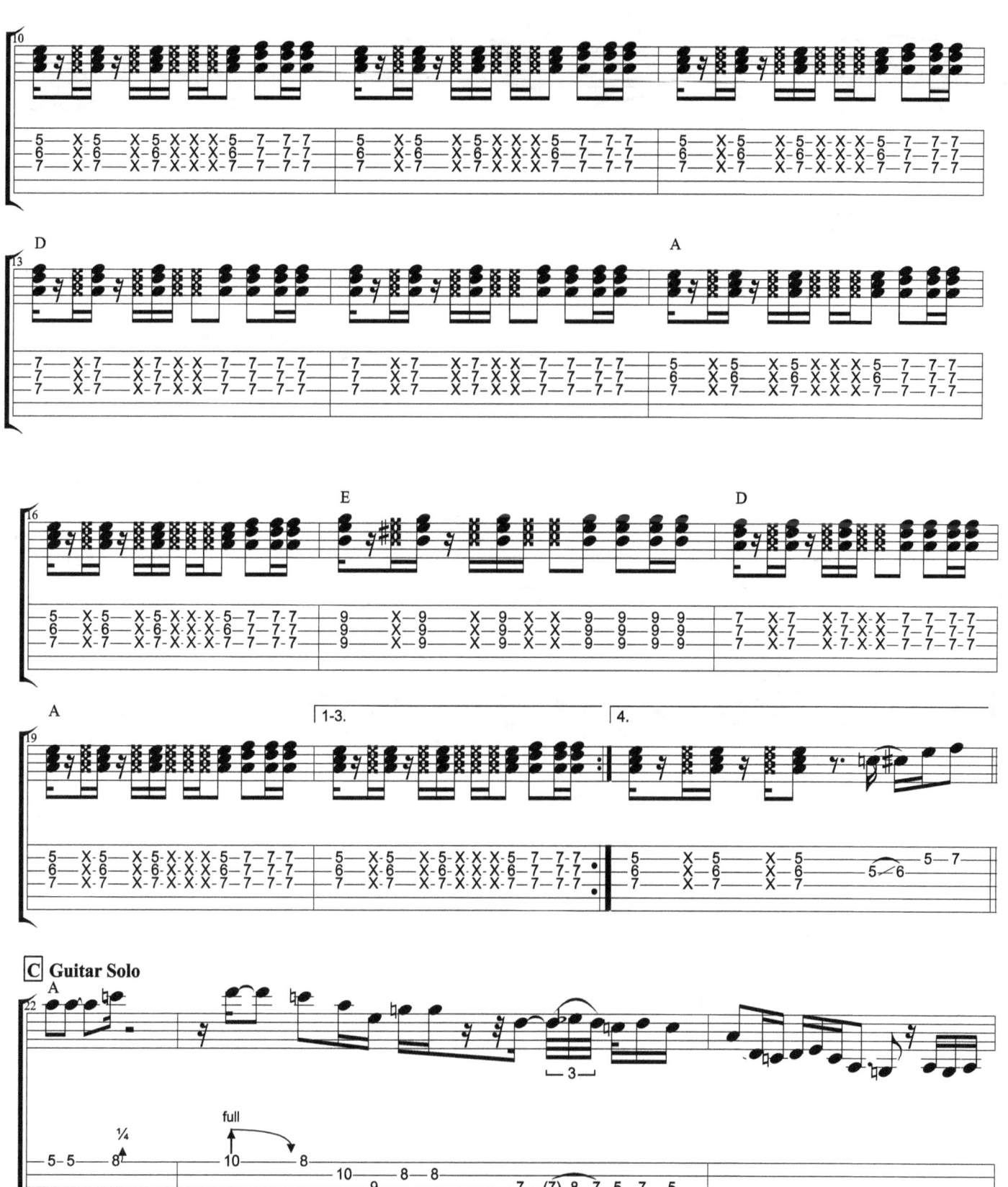

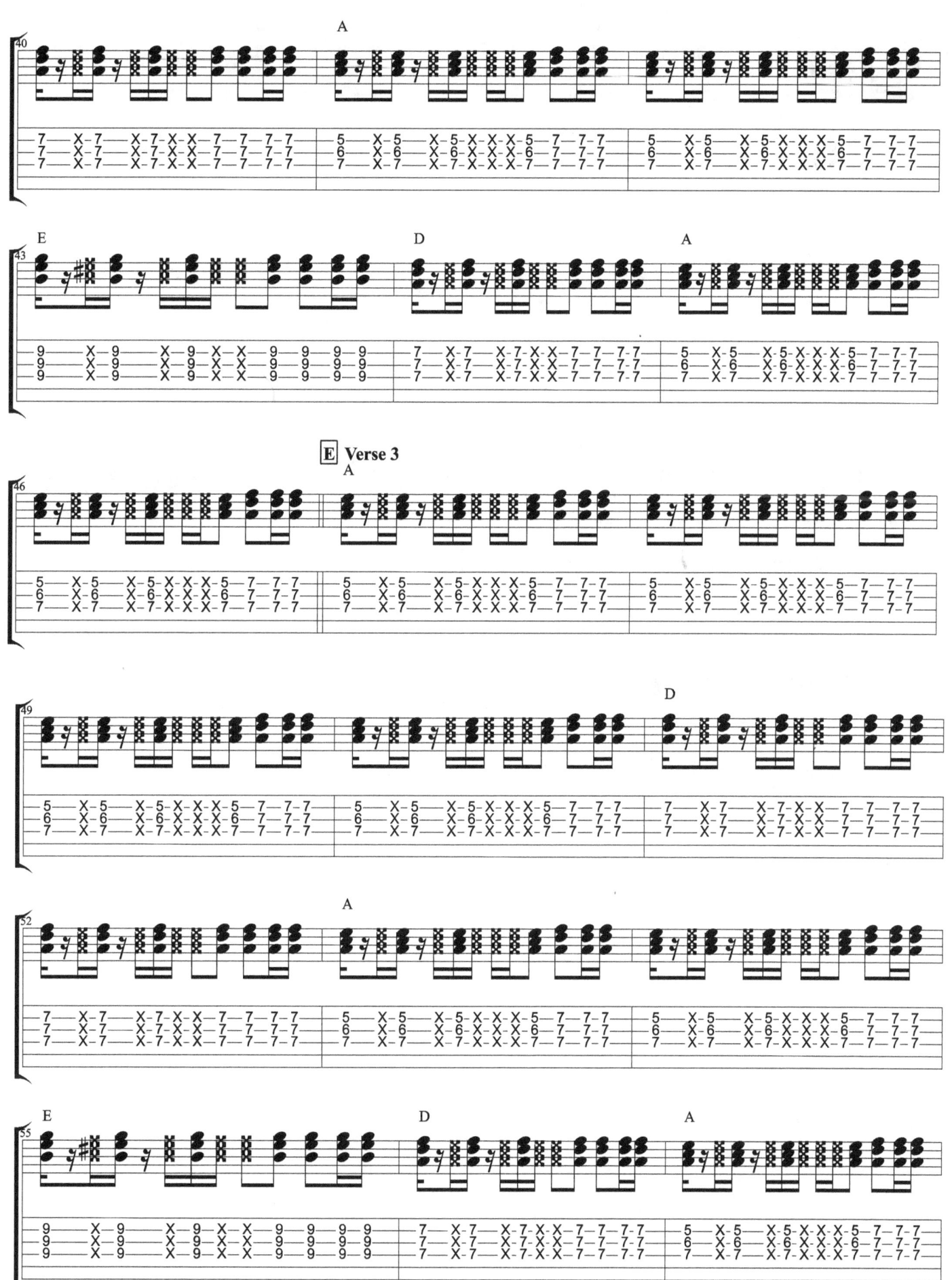

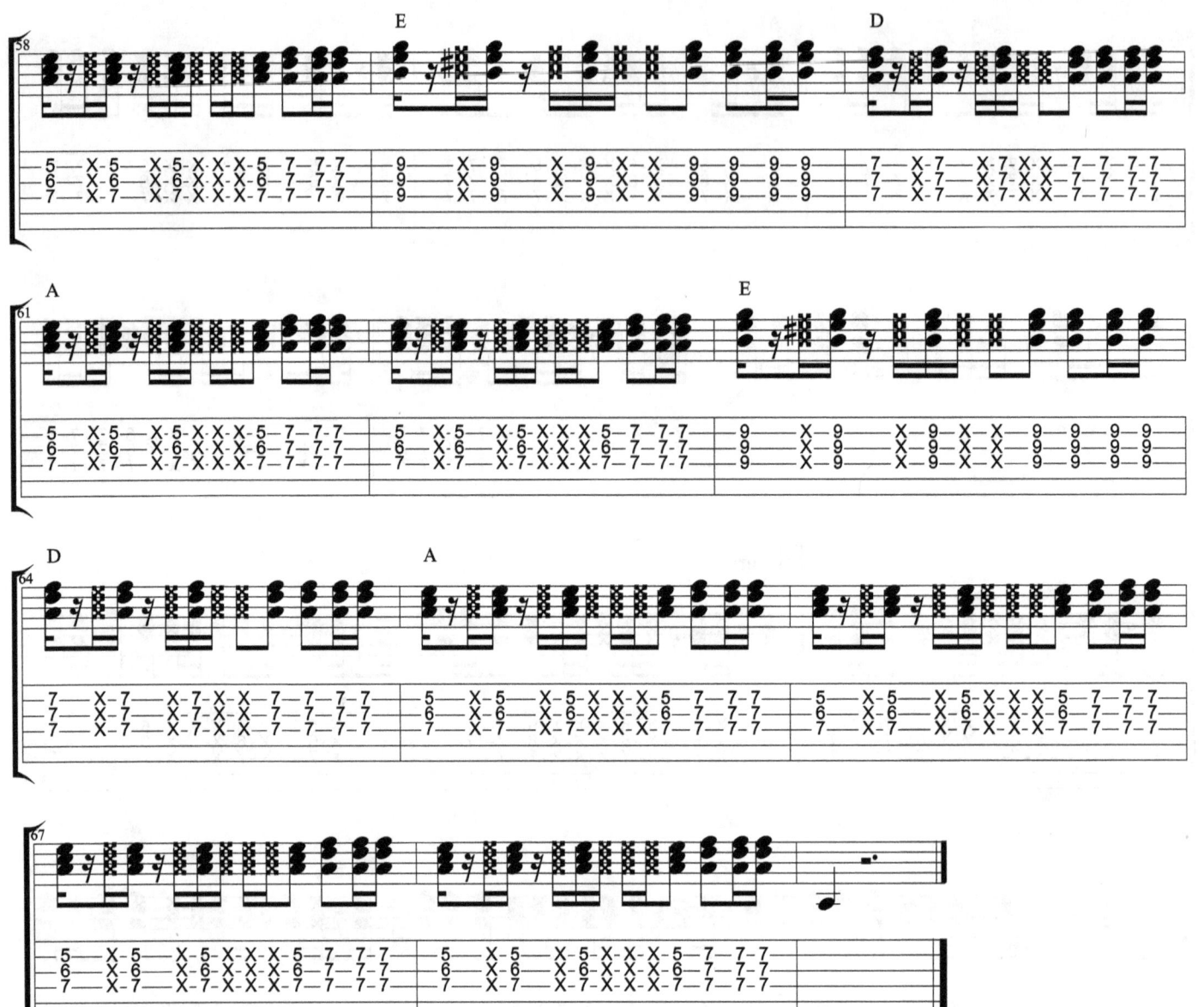

Steamrolled

This song has a 12 bar blues chord progression but the groove is more of a rock sort of thing that we worked out in the studio. The original groove that I had worked up was a little too generic feeling and we pretty much rewrote all of the parts in the studio to get what you have here.

Under the keyboard solo I play single notes to break up the arrangement and to give the solo a little bit more room. My guitar solo is a pretty straightforward blues rock/pentatonic lead through a fuzz pedal.

Pop!

This was the first song we played when we started rehearsing for the recording and it set a great vibe for everything else. I really wanted a funky instrumental in the Meters/John Scofield vein on the album and this is what I came up with.

The structure is *almost* a 12 bar blues for the "Head" or A section with a bridge that really takes you out of the G blues vibe for a little bit before returning to the head riff at the end. For soloing a "chorus" for each guy to solo over includes the whole A section and the bridge.

The main riff is alternate picked as much as possible but any place you see chords or parts with more than one note at a time you'll need to hybrid pick (as usual).

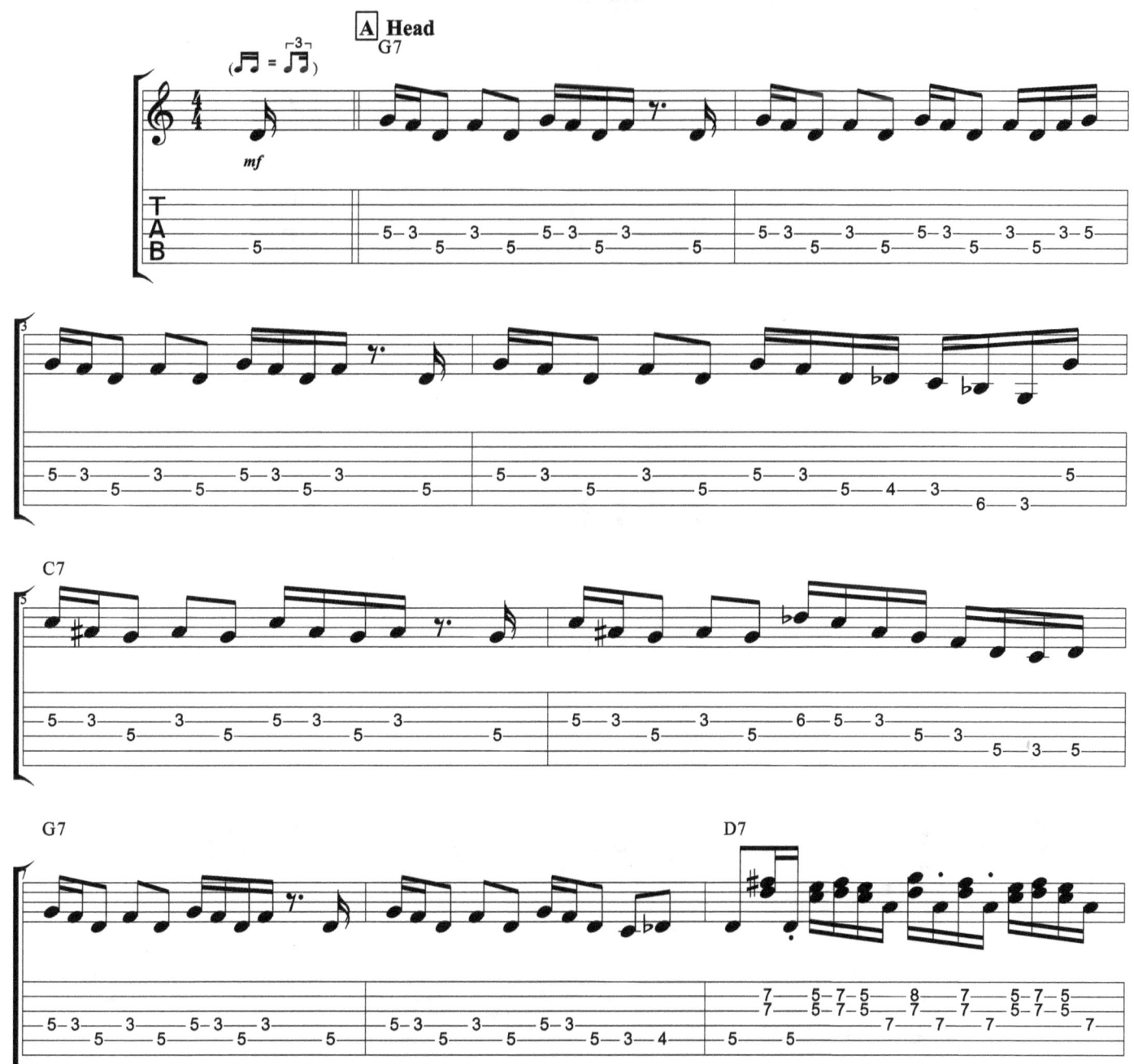

C7
D7
full
C7
G7
Bm7
C13
C7
Bm7
C7
Bm7
C13
C7
D9(♯9)
A Guitar Solo
G7

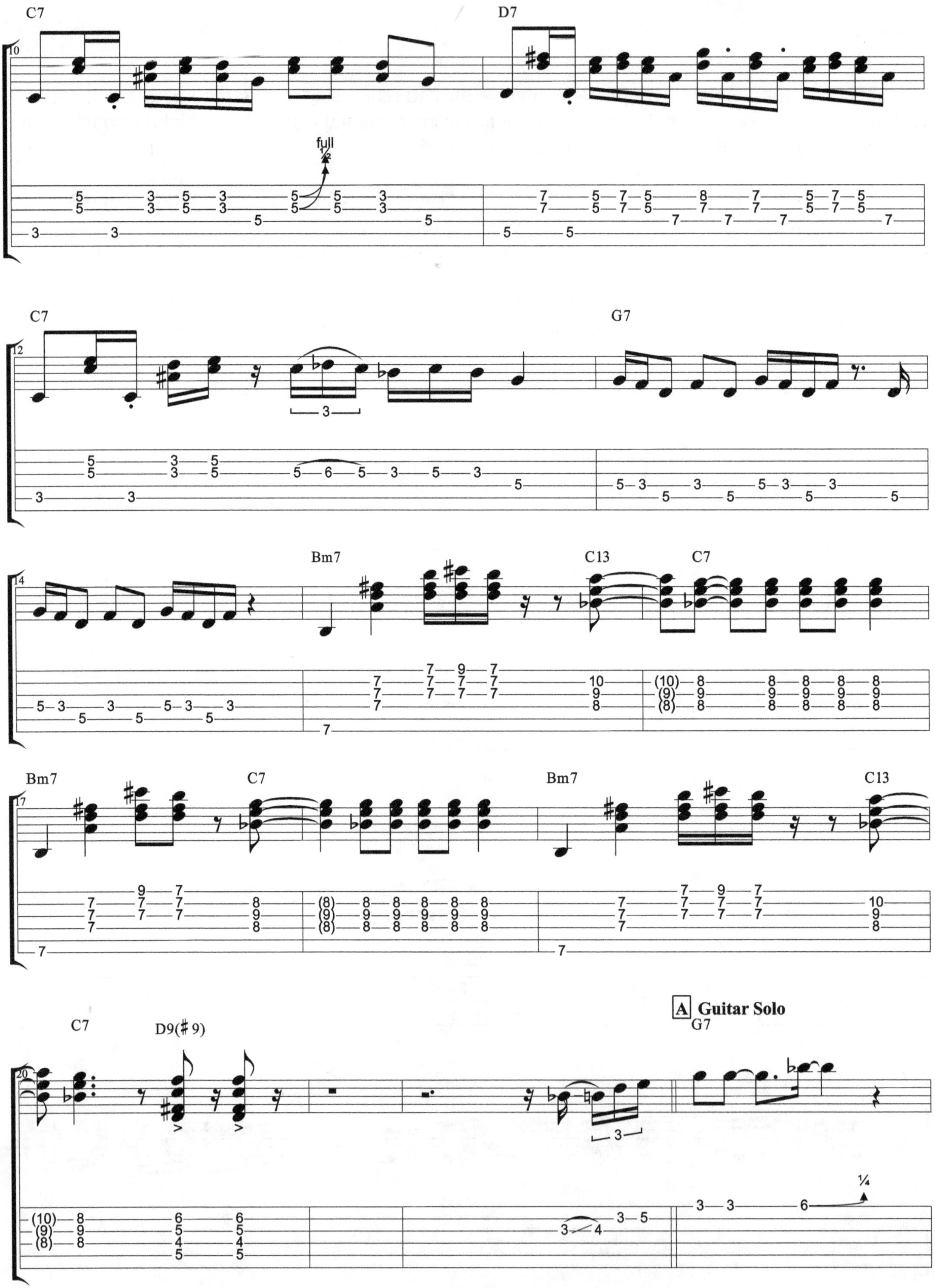

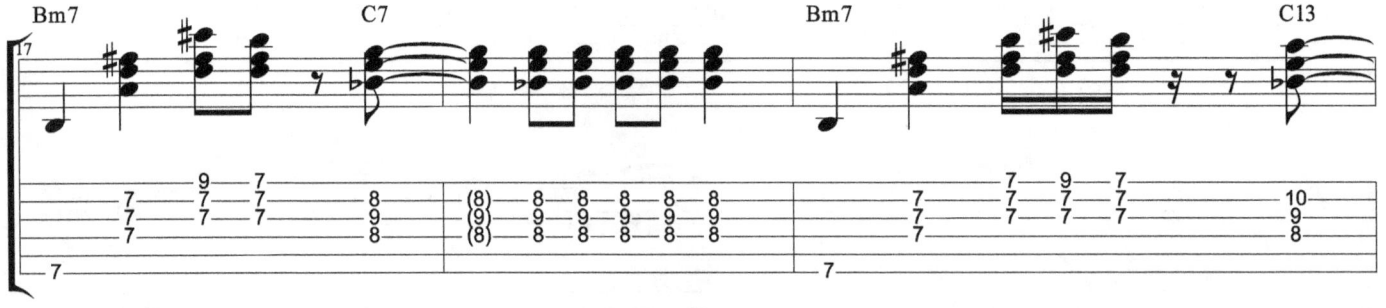

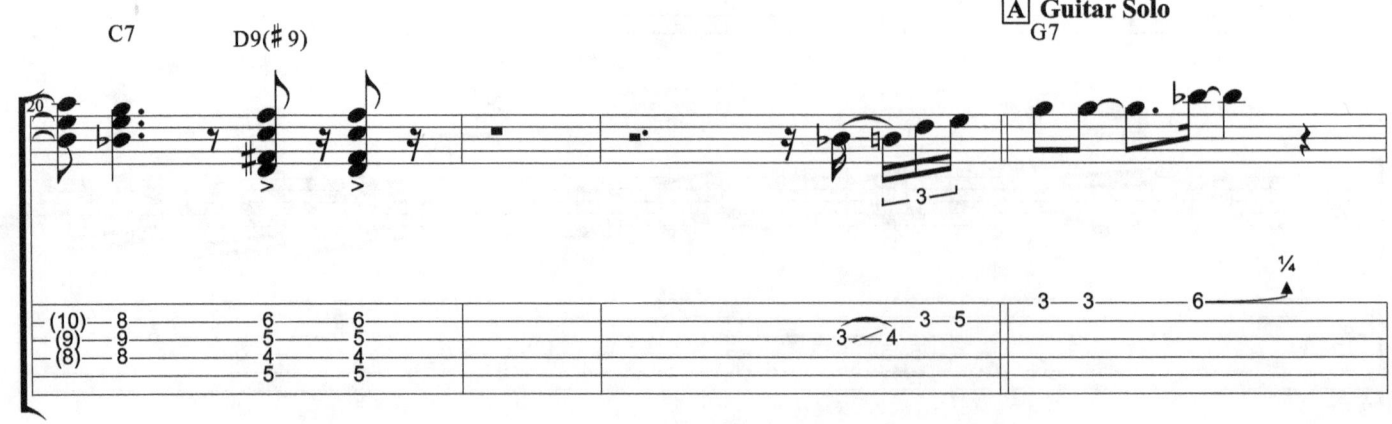

Everything's Cool

This song started life as a riff that I had come up with nearly 20 years ago for a funky Boogaloo version of Muddy Waters' song "Sugar Sweet". I've always loved the riff so when the opportunity to make this album came along I knew I had to write my own song around it.

The song is essentialy a Boogaloo guitar part played over a James Brown-style drum groove. Since I almost always played this song in single guitar bands I had combined the top and bottom parts for the Boogaloo into a composite riff with the backbeat chord stab added into the single note bottom part. In this recording we added a second guitar part played by Tommy Harkenrider to fill things in even more. That lesson is after the main transcription for my part. The song itself is a 12 bar blues in A. There is a breakdown part before the keyboard solo that breaks up the arrangement a little and the outro is a big dumb rock solo over F, G and Am (kind of like "Stairway to Heaven" played backwards).

The rhythm part for everything up to the outro solo was played on Scotts' 1972 Telecaster with super high action. Because of how difficult the guitar was to play I had to really beat the crap out of it to play the part solidly. I really liked the sound of the guitar AND the feel of the part so we kept that but I did recut the outro solo later on.

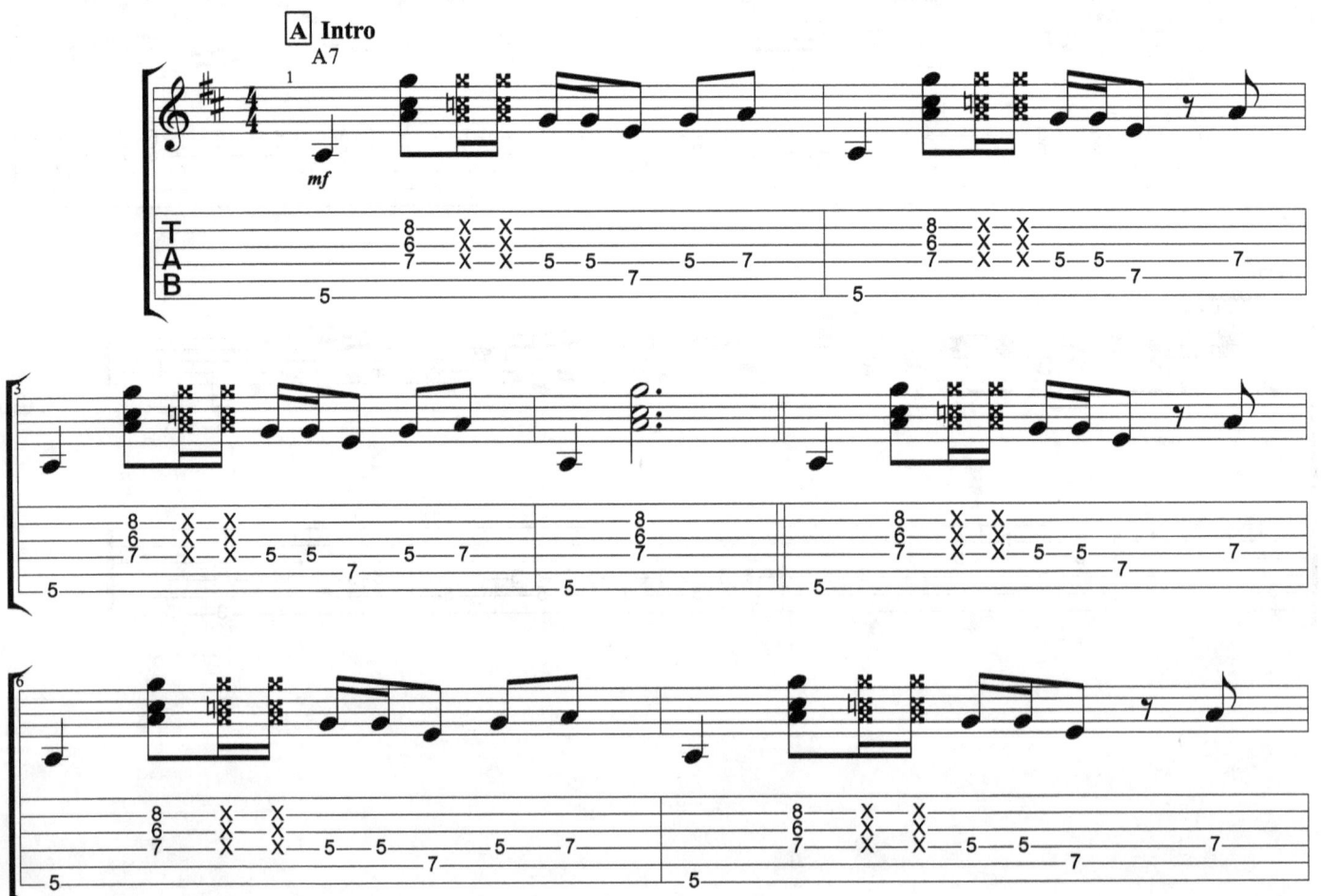

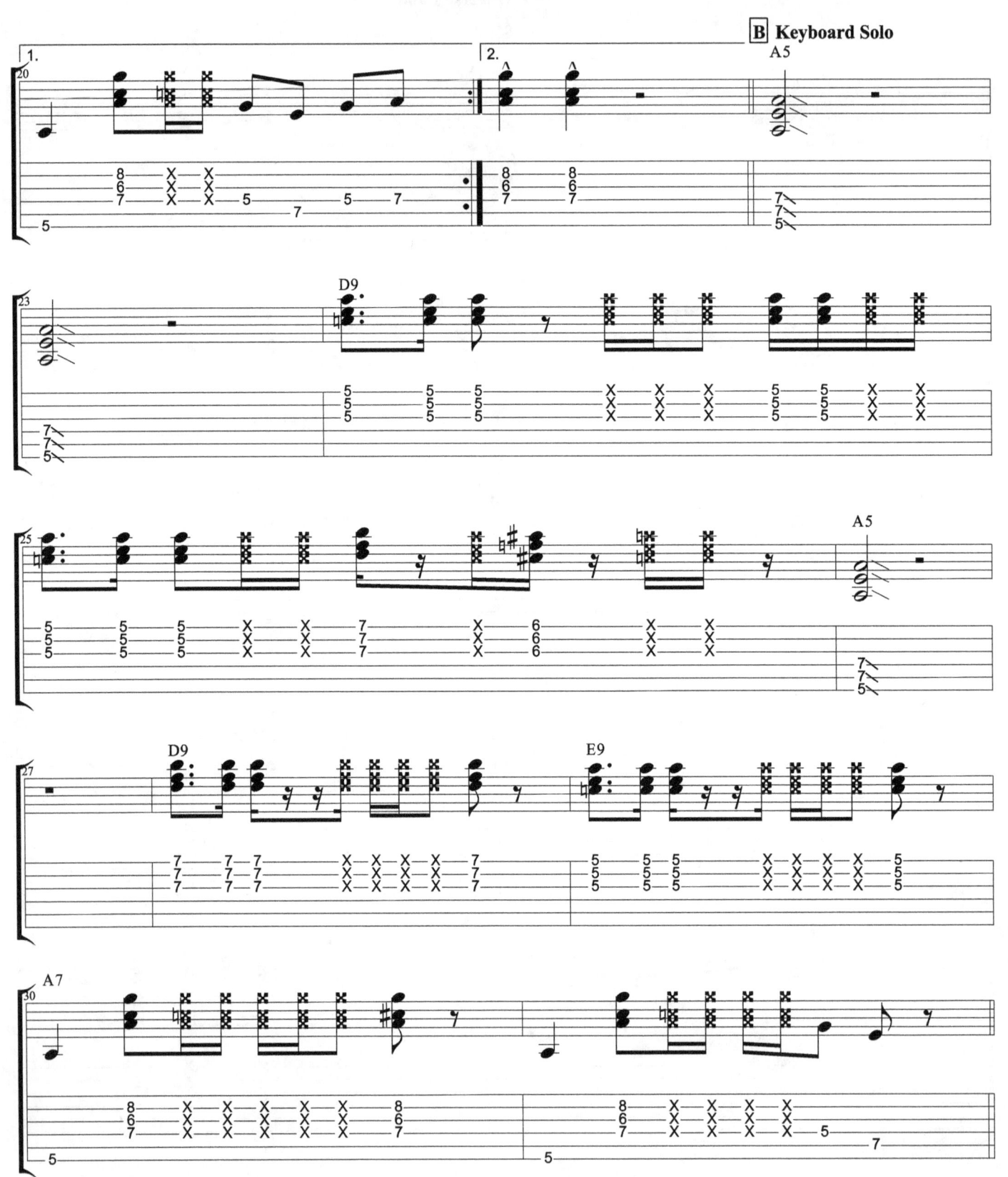

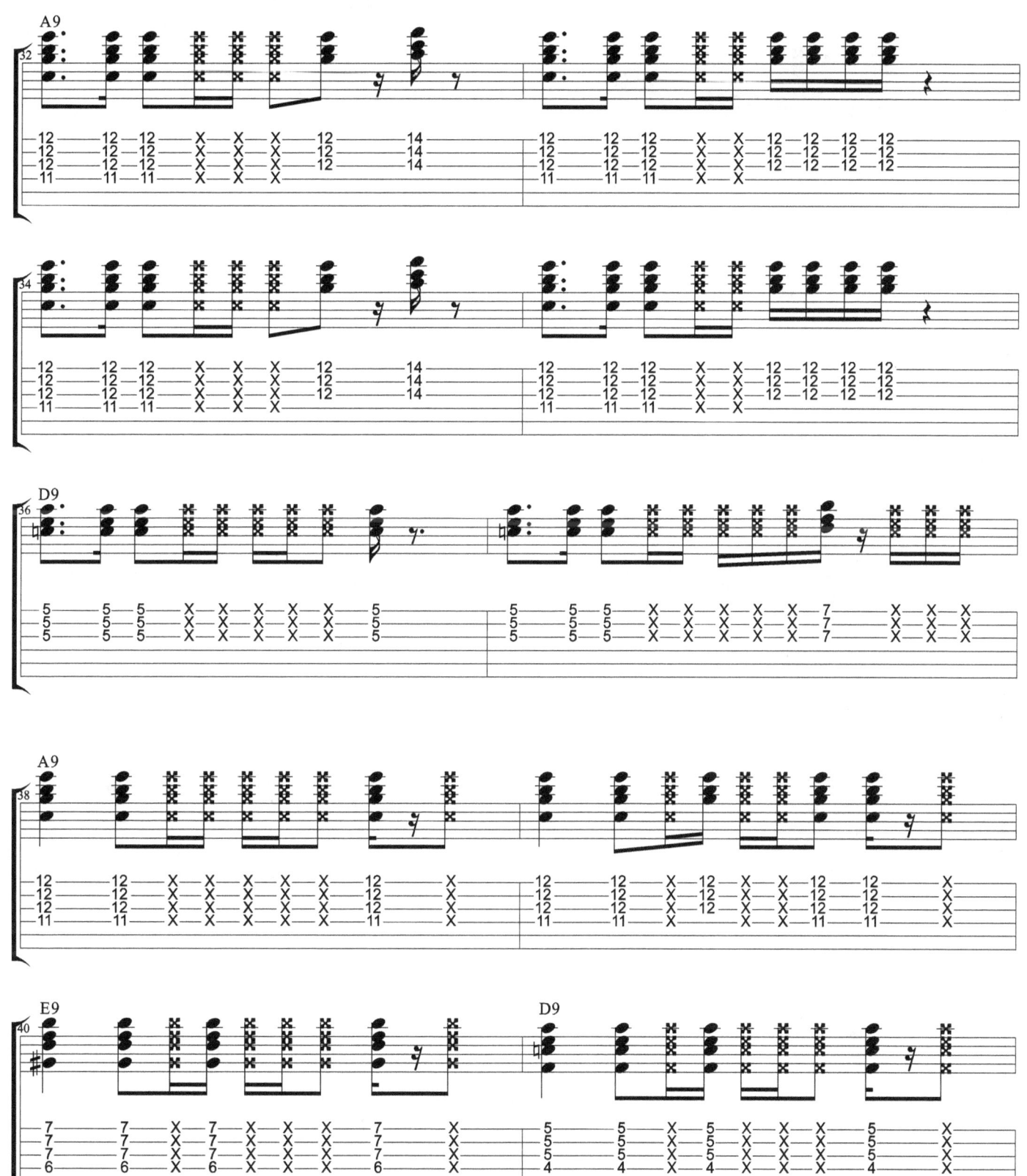

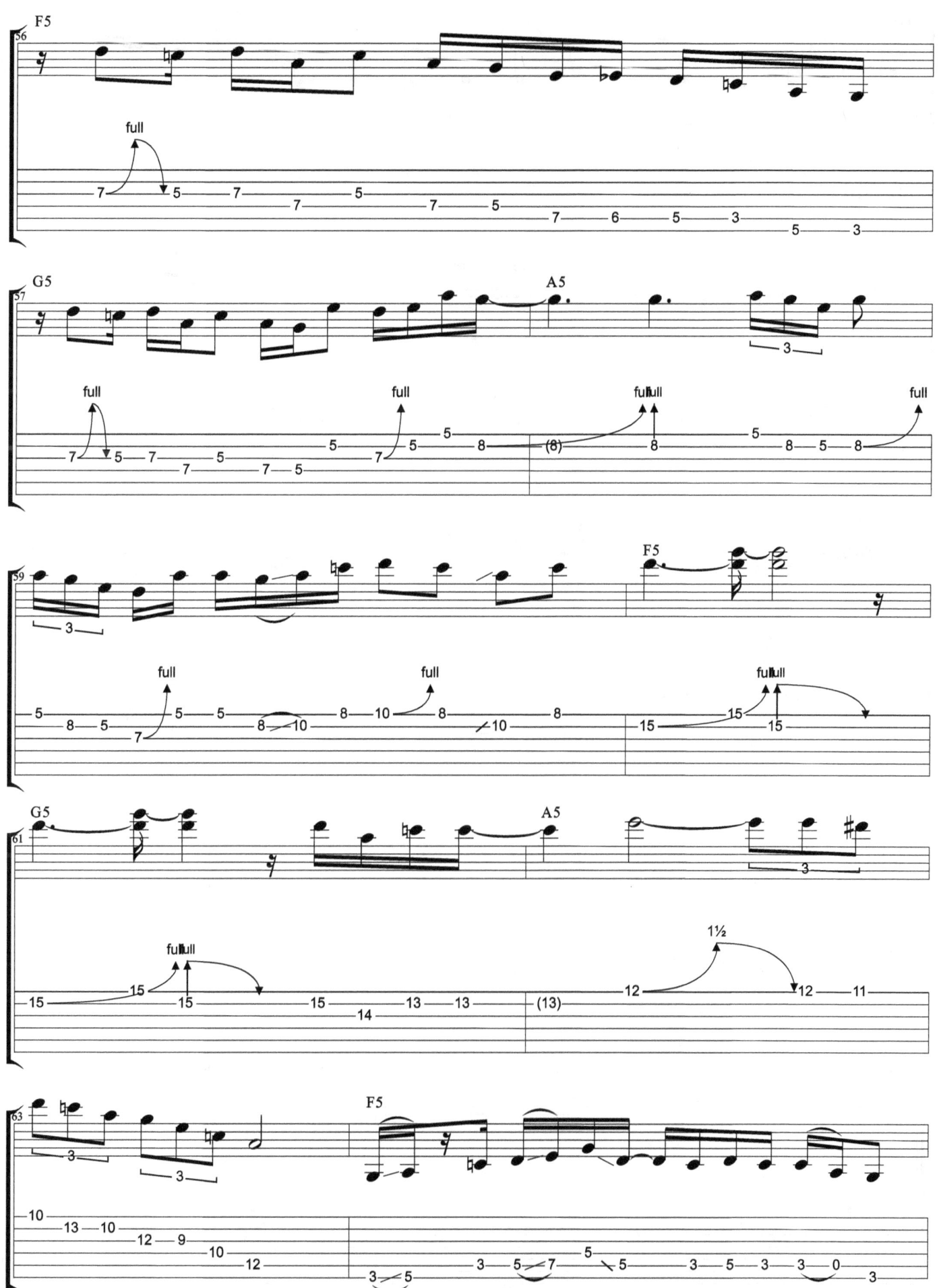

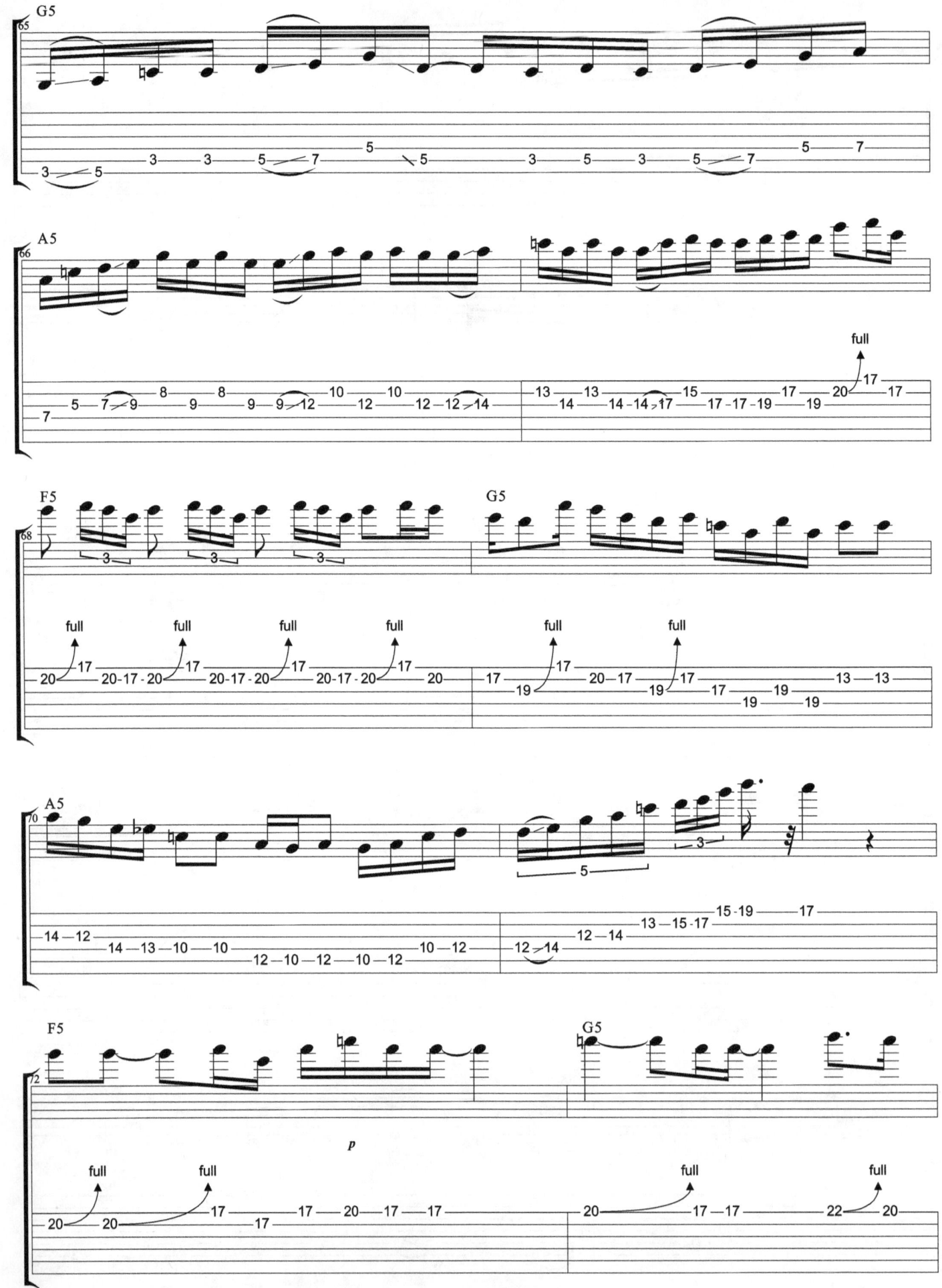

Toms' Guitar Part for "Everythings' Cool"

This is another song where a simple backbeat-type part completed the more complicated groove that I'm playing in my part. Tom Harkenrider is playing on beats 2, the "and" of 4 and the 2nd beat of the next measure until the 9th bar where he goes back to straight 2 and 4.

Under the solo at the end of the song his part switches to straight eighth notes with power chords until the end of the song.

120

Rhythm Guitar for "The Last Time"

The rhythm guitar part for this song is a Scotty Moore-type hybrid picking figure. Most folks will play this with a thumbpick and fingers but I hybrid prick with my pick, middle and ring fingers. In the examples below we will stick to the classical guitar conventions of "**P**" for the thumb (or in this case the pick), "**I**" for index finger (which will not be used since its also holding the pick), "**M**" for middle and "**A**" for your ring finger.

Here is the main rhythm figure for the I chord. It actually uses three different chords to complete the figure but we are considering the whole two measure phrase as the I chord. One other thing to consider is that this is in 2/2 or "cut time" so there are two counts to the measure. I will write the counting under the music and the right hand fingering under that. It is highly recommended that you do this slowly with a metronome until you can execute it cleanly.

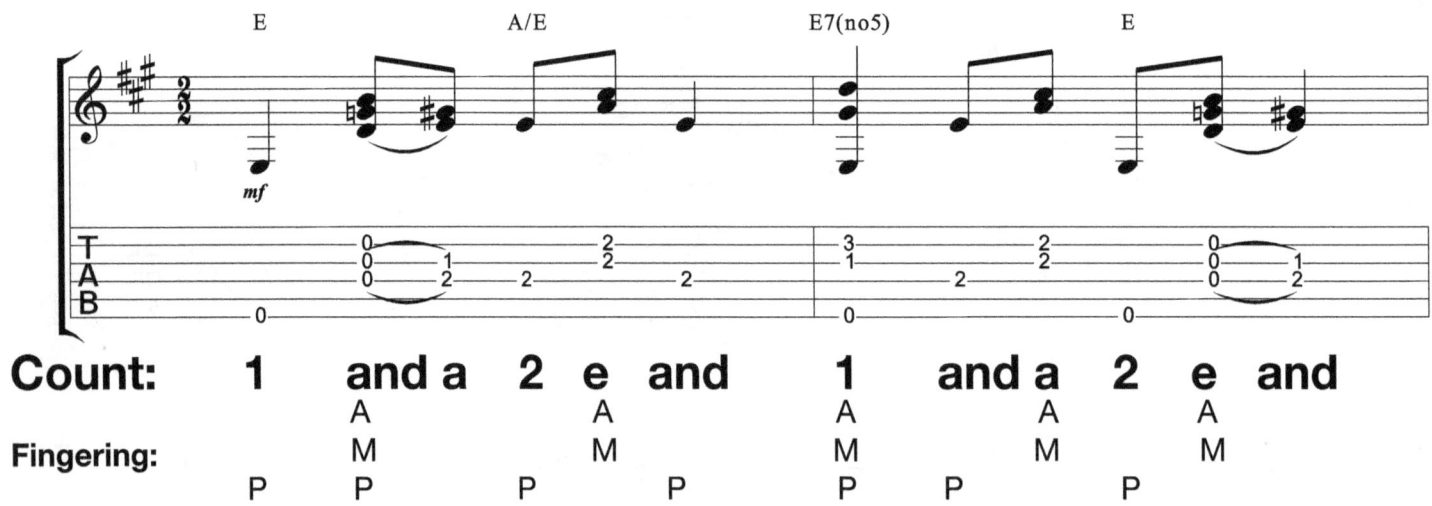

Figures for the IV and V chords:

122

Example for the Bridge:

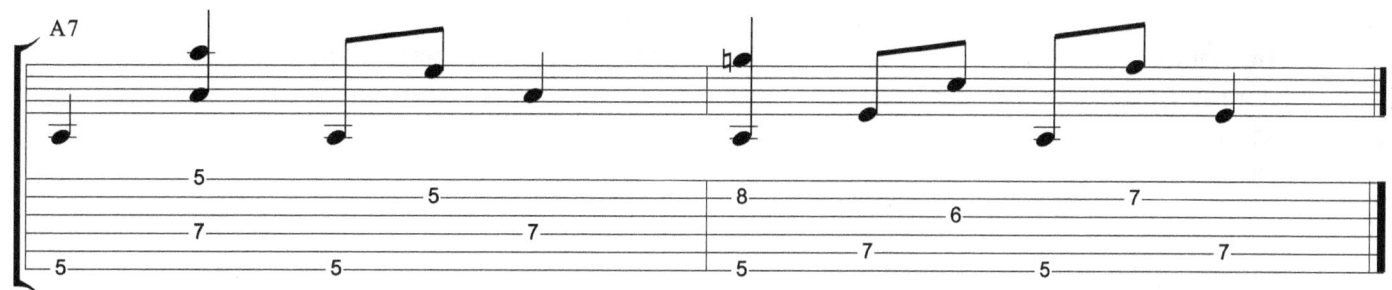

1 and **2** e and **1** and a **2** e and
    A   A   A   A
                                                M
P   P   P   P   P   P   P   P

The Last Time - Solo Examples

The solo in "The Last Time" has all of my favorite country guitar licks in it. Actually I think it has ALL of my country guitar licks in it. Most of the are fairly straighforward in execution but here are five ideas that I'd like to specify the right hand picking on.

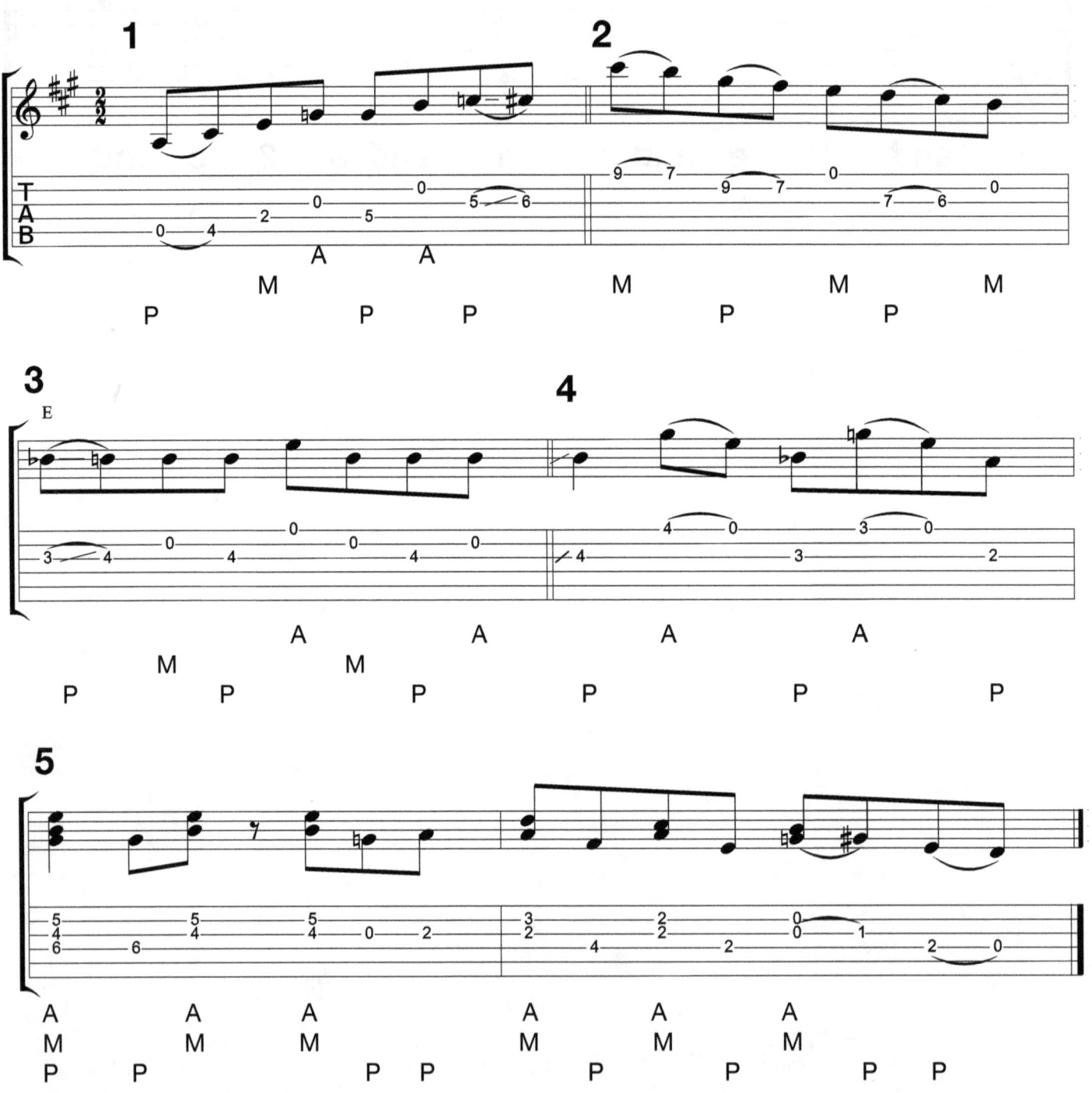

The Last Time - Acoustic Guitar

The acoustic guitar track just fills in space under the electric guitar on this song and keeps the track from feeling empty. It is a pretty standard "Boom-chick" (all down strum) sort of rhythm where you play the bass note of the chord alternating with the rest of the notes of the chord shape.

The Last Time

This song is less of a blues and more of a Rockabilly/Country tune but it is a ton of fun to play and I just really enjoy the song so we included it on the album. As you can tell from the last couple of pages you need to brush up on your hybrid picking skills to make it through this one. Try working each part out SLOWLY with a metronome before playing the song up to speed.

The solo goes by pretty quickly but you can slow it down and work each bar out pretty easily since I play pretty even subdivisions of time throughout the whole thing. Where there are oblique bends be extra careful to do them in tune. With most of the blues stuff that we play you can always play around with the pitch on a bend but in this style and especially with the oblique bends you need to be super accurate.

The guitar tone is pretty different on this one from the rest of the album. I'm playing a Suhr Tele-style guitar through a Silverface Princeton Reverb with a compressor pedal pretty cranked up for the electric parts and I am playing a Recording King steel string guitar for the only acoustic guitar track on the album.

The Last Time - Acoustic Guitar

The acoustic guitar track just fills in space under the electric guitar on this song and keeps the track from feeling empty. It is a pretty standard "Boom-chick" (all down strum) sort of rhythm where you play the bass note of the chord alternating with the rest of the notes of the chord shape.

The Last Time

This song is less of a blues and more of a Rockabilly/Country tune but it is a ton of fun to play and I just really enjoy the song so we included it on the album. As you can tell from the last couple of pages you need to brush up on your hybrid picking skills to make it through this one. Try working each part out SLOWLY with a metronome before playing the song up to speed.

The solo goes by pretty quickly but you can slow it down and work each bar out pretty easily since I play pretty even subdivisions of time throughout the whole thing. Where there are oblique bends be extra careful to do them in tune. With most of the blues stuff that we play you can always play around with the pitch on a bend but in this style and especially with the oblique bends you need to be super accurate.

The guitar tone is pretty different on this one from the rest of the album. I'm playing a Suhr Tele-style guitar through a Silverface Princeton Reverb with a compressor pedal pretty cranked up for the electric parts and I am playing a Recording King steel string guitar for the only acoustic guitar track on the album.

Subterrania (The Prize)

This song is a Minor Blues with a Dominant 7th IV chord.

> i chord for 4 measures
>
> IV chord for 2 measures
>
> i chord for 2 measures
>
> v chord for one measure
>
> iv chord for one measure
>
> i chord for two measures

The riff for both the i and IV chords is the same thing, with the change coming from the Bass and Keyboard parts. The song is in Bbm and the solos are pretty much my minor rock bag of licks through a phaser pedal.

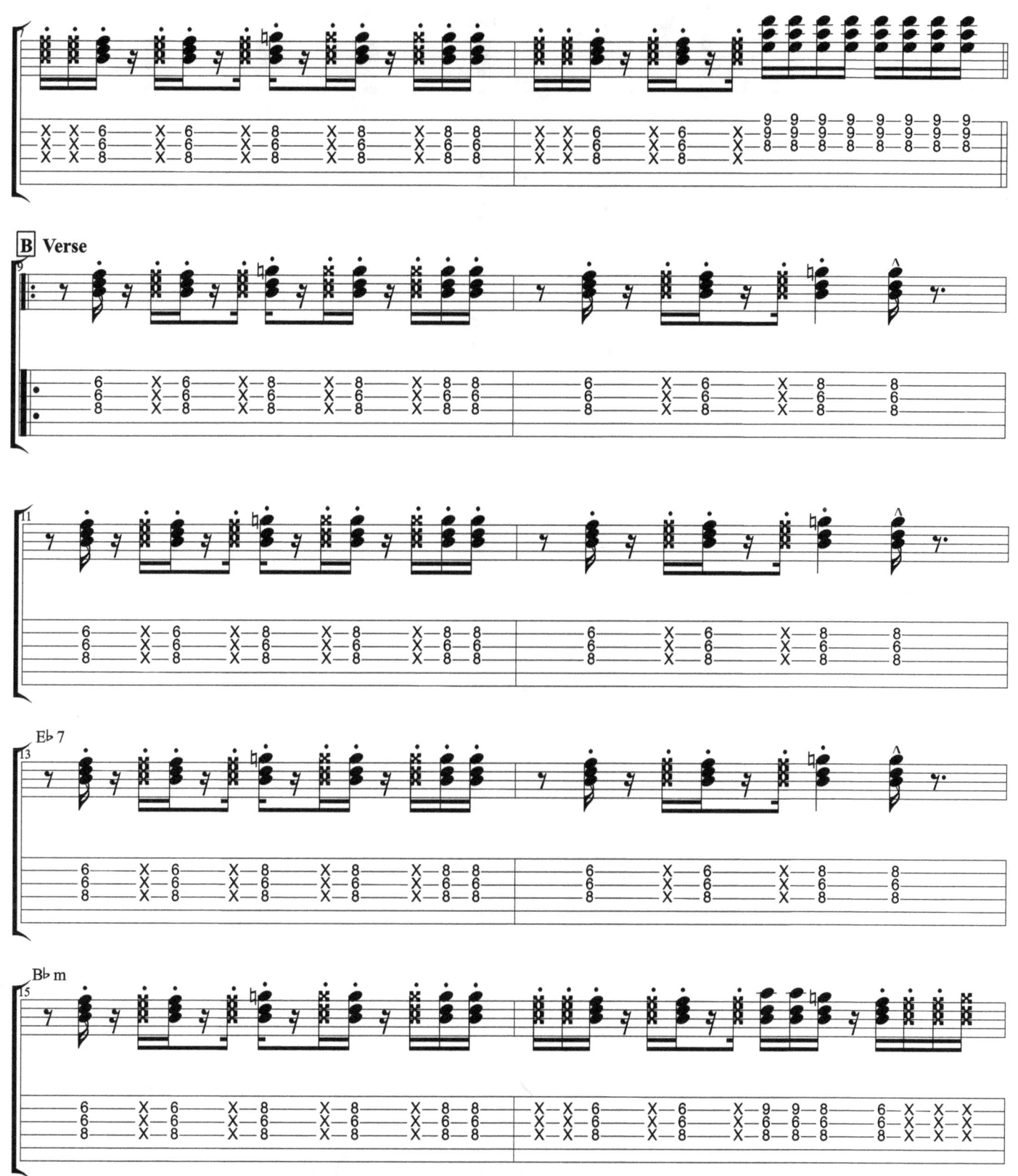

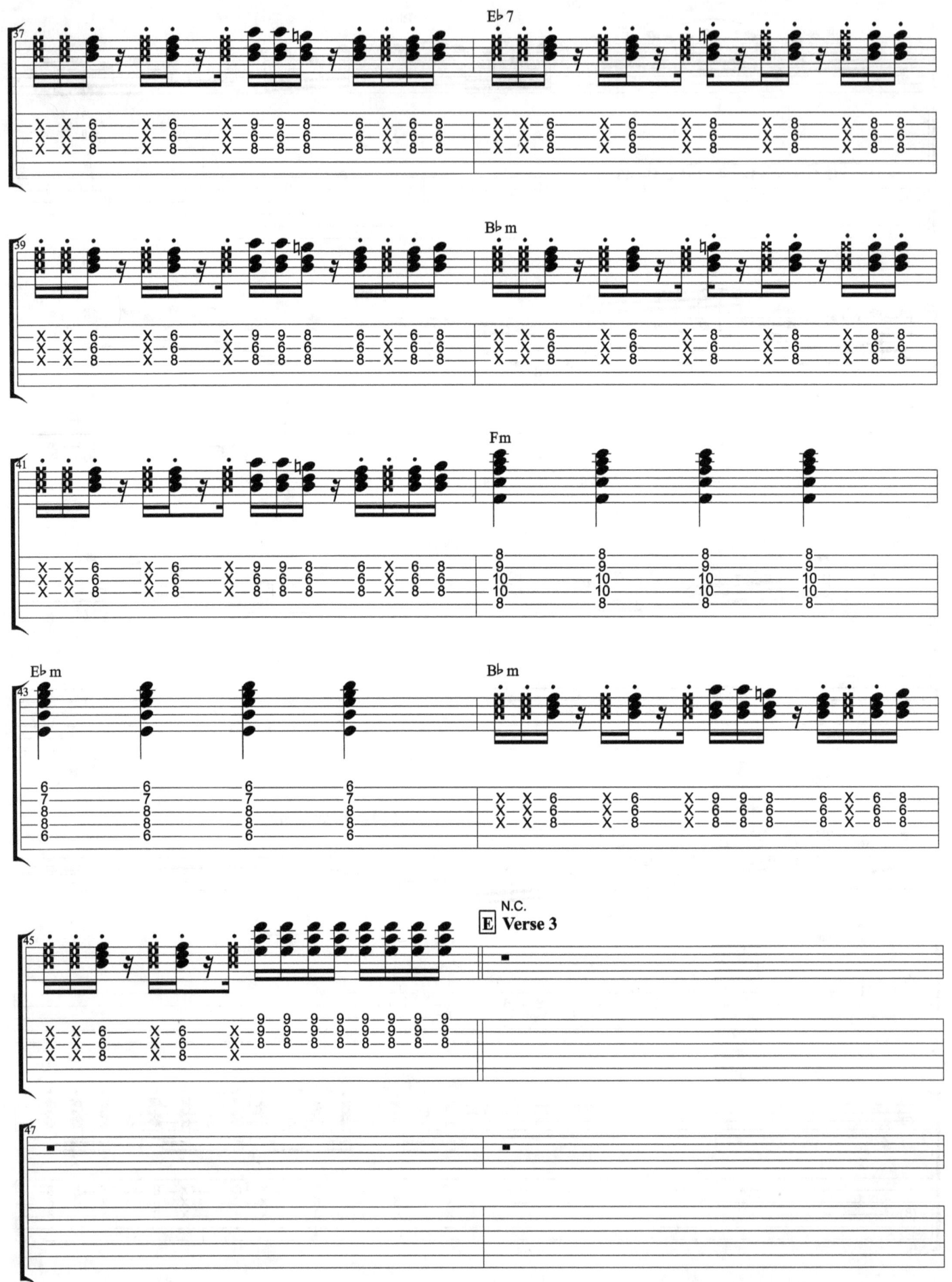

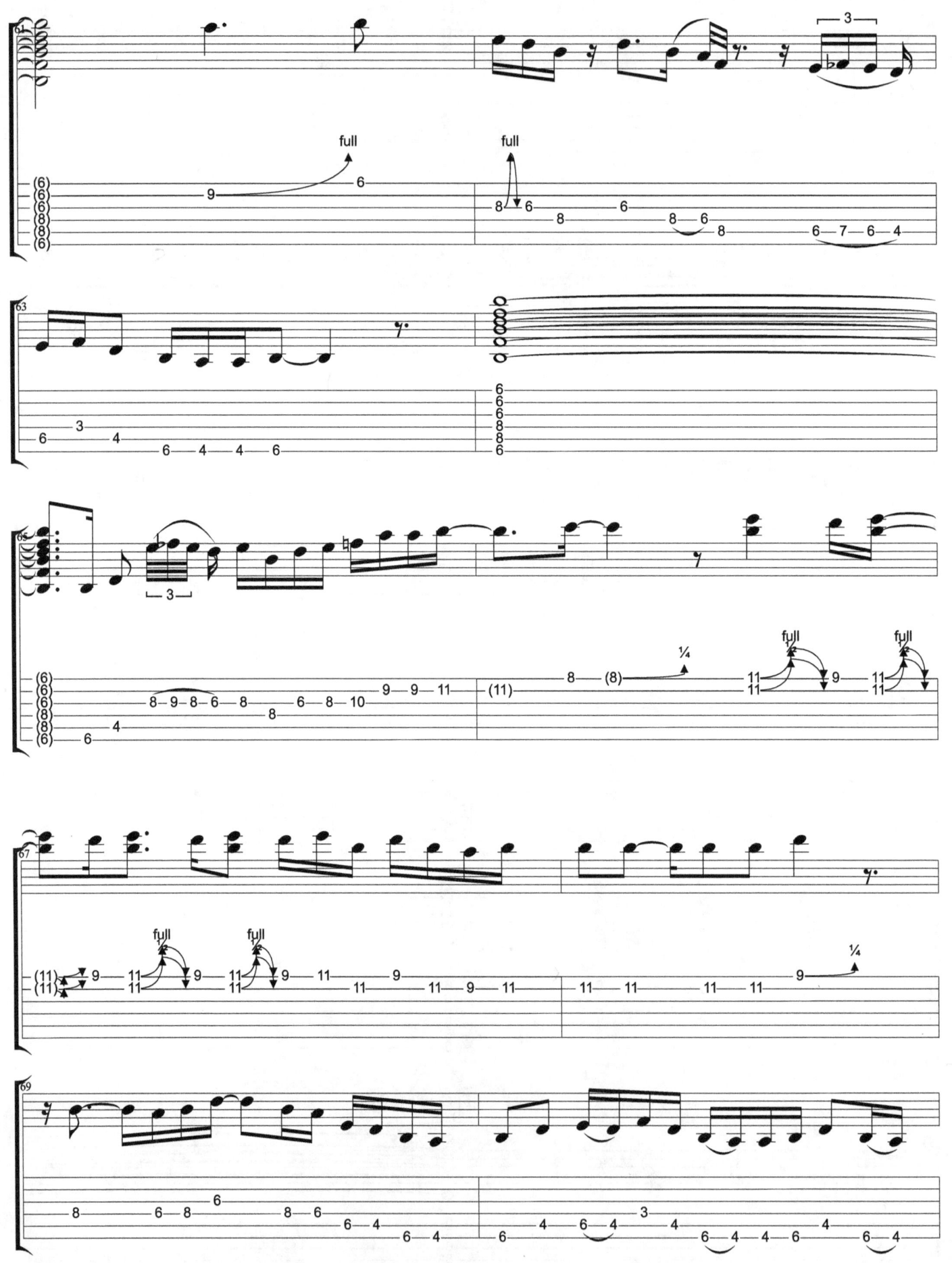

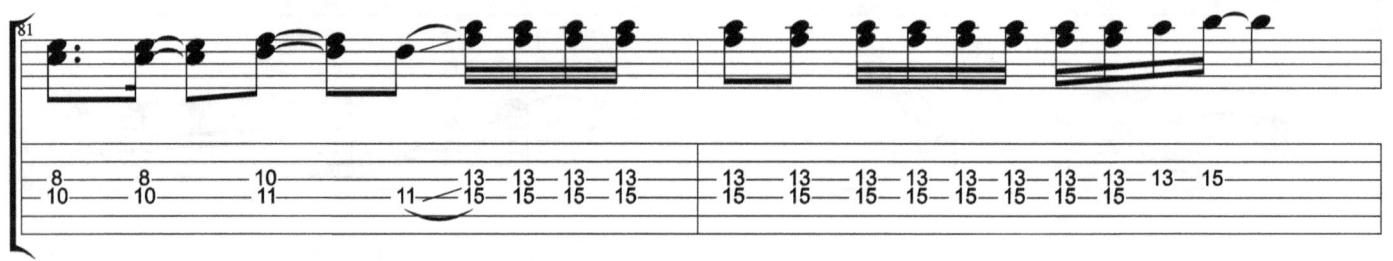
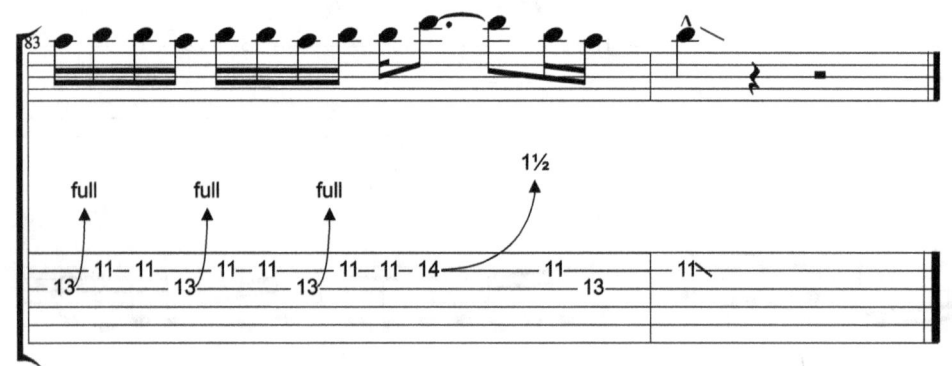

Now Available on iTunes, Amazon.com, CDbaby.com and pretty much anywhere else you can purchase music online!

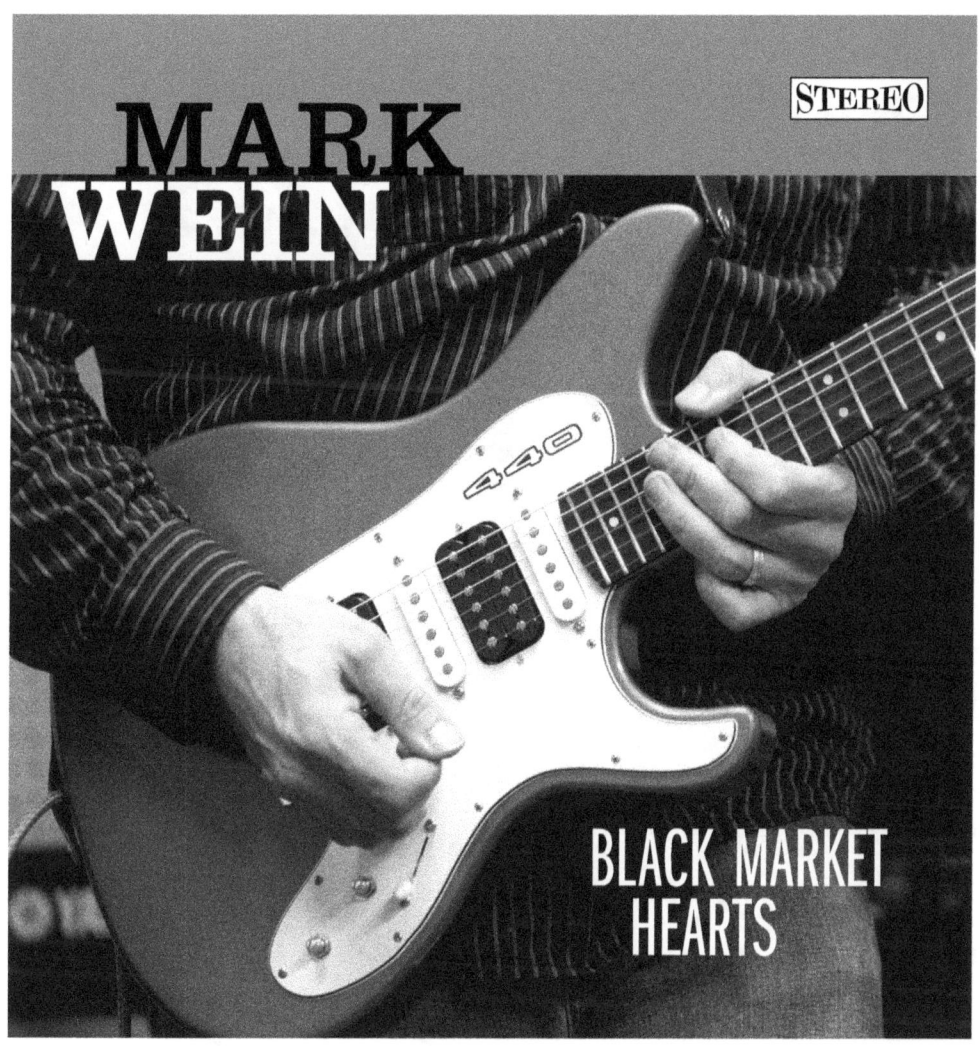

For more information and lesson material check out:

MarkWeinGuitarLessons.com

MarkWein.com

PremierSchoolofMusic.com

www.ingramcontent.com/pod-product-compliance
Lightning Source LLC
Chambersburg PA
CBHW080513110426
42742CB00017B/3105